Excellent words for every ⌐ _____ wonderful opportunity to be educated and prepared to share these truths with others.

> —**Randy Alcorn,** bestselling author of
> *Heaven* and *Giving Is the Good Life*

Christians, pro-choice or pro-life, will gain a renewed mindset about abortion.

> —**Katha D. Blackwell,** MSW, *Not Another Victim*

This thoughtful book answers the question, "Is God pro-choice or pro-life?"

> —**Kim de Blecourt,** author of *Until We All*
> *Come Home* and *I Call You Mine*

With grace and truth, the authors bring clarity to the Christian conundrum about abortion.

> —**Lynn Cory** is leader of Neighborhood Initiative and
> author of *Neighborhood Initiative and the Love of God*

In this challenging and timely book, Hammond and LaBonte point out that more than half of the abortions performed in the United States in a given year are obtained by those who identify themselves as Christians.

—**Craig von Buseck,** Author and Editor of Inspiration.org

Everyone has been told all we need is love, but what the world really needs is truth. This book forces us to see clearly the decision before all who claim to be followers of Jesus Christ.

—**Rick Burgess,** co-host of *The Rick and Bubba Show* and *New York Times* bestselling author and speaker

Through this book, the authors show why the Church must get more involved. We may be able to give diverse opinions on many issues, but abortion is not one of these issues.

—**Scott Dawson,** former candidate for Governor of Alabama, founder of Strength to Stand Student Conferences, and CEO of Scott Dawson Evangelistic Association, Inc.

To Roger Proclaim the Truth [signature]

THE CHRISTIAN AND ABORTION

A *Nonnegotiable* Stance

STEVE HAMMOND, MD
AND EMILY LABONTE, FNP-BC

credo
house publishers

Published in the United States by Credo House Publishers,
a division of Credo Communications LLC, Grand Rapids, Michigan
credohousepublishers.com

ISBN: 978-1-62586-142-9

Cover and interior design by Frank Gutbrod
Editing by Donna Huisjen

Printed in the United States of America
First edition

CONTENTS

Preface *1*

1. A Young Doctor's Story *17*
2. When Does Life Begin? *27*
3. A Mother's View on When Life Begins *39*
4. How Does God View Abortion? *55*
5. Sanctity of Life and Related Topics *65*
6. When Things Go Wrong *83*
7. The Truth about the Lies Women Are Told *97*
8. Whose Rights? *115*
9. Dany's Story *119*
10. Kermit Gosnell *129*
11. Adoption *133*
12. Kelcey's Story *139*
13. So What Should a Christian Do? *147*
14. Closing Prayer and Thoughts *157*

Appendix A: Fetal Development Chart *161*
Appendix B: Resources *162*
Acknowledgments *164*
Endnotes *166*

PREFACE

Emily LaBonte, FNP-BC

While I was in church on Sunday morning, March 26, 2017, I began to feel very uncomfortable. My heart started racing, and I started feeling pressure in my chest that was similar to what people describe having during a major cardiac event. I could not stop squirming in my chair. I've learned that people experience the Holy Spirit in many different ways, and from my own past encounters I knew what was happening. I was so distracted by the Holy Spirit that I could not listen to that morning's sermon. I felt the Holy Spirit begin to flood my mind with information about abortion, Scripture on the sanctity of life, questions that people have surrounding abortion, and reasons why women have abortions. As I sat in church, I knew without a doubt that the Lord was calling me to write a book about why Christians should be pro-life.

I started doing my research and looking into different resources because, as a healthcare professional and a Christian, I knew it is important that I include information for readers that is both theologically and medically sound. A few weeks after starting this process, I called an OB/GYN friend from Tennessee to see if he had any resources for me in my endeavors to do research for this book, such as textbooks on abortion procedures, scientific evidence of life in the womb, etc. He then put me in touch with Dr. Steve Hammond, one of his OB/GYN partners at his practice, and said that Dr. Hammond would be able to serve me better and give me a remarkable perspective because he had been an abortionist at one time.

I learned that the Lord had been working in Dr. Hammond's life for years to bring him to the point of writing a book on the same topic, and the relationship of co-authorship took flight the first time we spoke. Dr. Hammond told me to listen to a sermon that his church—Fellowship Bible Church in Jackson, Tennessee—had recently presented on the sanctity of life. Dr. Hammond's pastor had included him in the discussion around the sanctity of life and fetal development, and he had asked him to share his personal testimony. As I listened to the sermon, I was astounded by its truth and boldness. And then I learned the most amazing thing: the sermon date was March 26, 2017—the very same day that I had felt the Lord call me to write this book. This was certainly no coincidence, and ever since I felt the call the Lord has orchestrated every step of the authorship of this book. Indeed, the Lord equips the called, and He confirms and reconfirms callings on our lives to bring to fruition what He is calling us to do.

Several months prior to March 2017 and meeting Dr. Hammond, an old friend with whom I worked at a church camp many years ago sparked a lengthy conversation on abortion, including the many different questions that people ask about abortion, excuses that people make to justify abortion, and Scripture surrounding abortion, among many other topics discussed. In doing my research on the subject, I came to find that there is an especially high incidence of Christians having abortions.

According to the Guttmacher Institute, 17 percent of abortion patients in 2014 identified themselves as mainline Protestant, 13 percent identified as evangelical Protestant, and 24 percent identified as Catholic.[1] In reality, this number may be even higher, as many respondents likely refused to claim their religion. This means that more than half of the abortions performed in the United States during 2014 were obtained by Christians. This honestly broke my heart. As an avid Christian who believes the biblical teachings on the sanctity of life, I asked myself why so many Christians are getting abortions. What if believers are being led astray by false theology or truly have not thought in depth about the sanctity of life? What if they truly do not know what God thinks about abortion? Second Timothy 4:3–4 says, "For the time is coming when people will not endure sound teaching, but having itching ears they will accumulate for themselves teachers to suit their own passions, and will turn away from listening to the truth and wander off into myths."

We live in a time that is so confusing. As authors Francis J. Beckwith and Gregory Koukl poignantly note, we live in a time of relativism, and our feet are firmly planted in mid-air. We live in a world that polarizes people who stand for pro-life principles against those who are "pro-choice." Our secular society does not believe in absolute truth. We live in a hedonistic world that tells us that if something feels right or is convenient, then we should do it. However, I will boldly assert that not everything that feels good is right under the standard of the one holy God, and there are absolute truths that we should not ignore. Human life is sacred to our God; it is actually worth dying for. Romans 5:8 says, "But God shows his love for us in that while we were still sinners, Christ died for us."

In this book we will explain how "pro-choice" is essentially a synonym for pro-abortion, as the outcome is the same—abortion on demand. As Beckwith and Koukl point out, "Saying 'if you don't like abortion, don't have one' to those opposed to abortion is similar to telling abolitionists not to own slaves if they don't like slavery."[2] Since *Roe v. Wade* in 1973, abortion has been and continues to be a very emotional topic. Activists from both sides have been passionate and even violent toward one another. We have seen some Protestant churches support or stand silent on the pro-abortion movement, often on the wings of feminism. In the following passage, R. C. Sproul gives detail to the "pro-choice" movement's strategy in the 1970s to get abortion legalized:

> At this same time, many of the mainline churches were involved in controversies on vital issues relating to feminism. . . . These sweeping gains had been won at painful cost, but many women were fearful that their gains were not secure. By linking the pro-choice position to that of pro-women, the pro-abortionists' strategy was effective in gaining widespread endorsement for pro-choice from Protestant denominations. In a vital sense, the pro-choice position rode the coattails of the pro-women position in the churches. Those who were struggling for the consolidation of women's rights in the church perceived that adopting the pro-choice position was critical, or the activism for other rights might be weakened.[3]

Many churches' support of the feminist movement started as a good thing; the church supported women fighting for equal rights. When feminists began beckoning the legal system to legalize abortion, many churches did not speak against it. This means that some churches either supported or did not stand against legalizing abortion in order to avoid impinging on women's rights. But what if this had never been labeled a women's rights issue to begin with? If you fast-forward to now, we see that there are feminist movements—such as Feminists for Life—that are pro-life and churches that are "pro-choice."

Because even the church has not been unified on an absolute moral truth, those truths have been clouded, and abortion is one of the many issues in the church that is being morally clouded. The truth is that the church is being secularized by culture instead of influencing culture through the Word of God. The church has not been able to become a force that demands truth and protection of the unborn because the church itself is not united. If the church cannot even agree, then who determines its values?

Unfortunately, politicians are determining what is legal, so many people view legality as morality, which simply is not the case. Part of the Great Commission involves teaching others to obey. In Matthew 28:19–20 Jesus says, "Go therefore and make disciples of all nations, baptizing them in the name of the Father and of the Son and of the Holy Spirit, teaching them to observe all that I have commanded you. And behold, I am with you always, to the end of the age."

I believe that obedience, in this case, means not having or performing abortions, so I believe that it is part of our Great Commission from God to teach others how and why to obey. This is why Dr. Hammond and I have such a burden for this topic. Christians are confused and do not know what to believe about abortion.

This book is not intended to condemn Christ-followers or judge those who have undergone or have performed abortions—I cannot stress this enough! We serve a God who forgives and redeems us, and by no means do I have the authority to judge anyone, as that right only belongs to the Lord. This book is intended to be a resource for Christians, enabling you to dive deeper into the topics mentioned above (and many others) and urging you to seriously ponder and pray about the sanctity of life and whether abortion is absolutely right or absolutely wrong—as it cannot be both. This book is meant to provide you with the information needed to make that decision, but I believe that only the Holy Spirit can change your mind.

As children of God, we know that He is not finished with us once we experience salvation. He is constantly working in our hearts to make us more like Him (through sanctification). If you are a believer and are pro-abortion, please pray and ask God if this is an area of your heart and life that needs to undergo sanctification. If you are pro-life, I pray that this book will be a thought-provoking resource for you.

Above all, I implore you, believer, to seek the Lord with all of your heart on this issue because I believe that we live in a time in which the greatest genocide of all history is occurring. Babies do not have voices to speak up and defend themselves, and it is time for us to speak up for the voiceless. This is why I believe that Christians must be unified and must speak up and be absolutely pro-life. It is time to rise and educate our culture about the truth of God's standard. God alone is the standard for righteousness and truth. That is why we write this book and ask you this question: Is the God of the Bible pro-abortion or pro-life . . . and what does that mean for you?

Steve Hammond, MD

When Emily and I began writing this book, the abortion controversy was on the back burner of most news organizations. The debate began in earnest when the Senate hearings for now Justice Kavanaugh were underway. Those favoring abortion opposed his nomination chiefly due to fear that he would be the swing vote that might doom Roe v. Wade.

In recent days the abortion debate has become so hyper-partisan that one can almost feel the heat emanating from the television screen. New York has instituted a state law that codifies abortion up until the moment of birth and in essence removes the protection of the baby born alive that might survive a late term abortion. It would be one thing if the law had simply been passed under the cloak of darkness, but Governor Cuomo proclaimed the announcement with pride to the cheering of the gathered audience in the state Senate chamber. In the state of Virginia, Governor Northam, himself a pediatrician, explained the details of a proposed bill before the state Legislature on a radio call in show. It would address the fate of a baby that survived a late term abortion attempt. He said, "The baby would be made comfortable while the woman and the doctor would decide what to do" (whether or not to offer life support). Several other states are considering similar measures. The response to these developments has led to cheers and celebration on one side, horror and disbelief on the other.

Within weeks of New York's announcement, Georgia passed a bill that would restrict abortion after a baby's heartbeat was detected on ultrasound. Several other states have passed or are considering passing similar measures. The response to this was swift and frenzied. Boycotts of the states were proposed. The bills were denounced by almost 200 CEOs as "bad for business." Several politicians called the measures "extreme," and "an assault on human rights." Some called the bill "immoral."

This leads us to see this debate in broader philosophical terms. Both sides have claimed a moral high ground proclaiming that their position is on the side of truth, morality, and righteousness. The premise of this book, and one that I hope to make plain in my chapters, is that only one side can possibly be on the side of absolute truth. One cannot condone abortion by default, claiming to be neutral, and at the same time support the sanctity of life. You have to choose.

Hopefully, some Christian pro-lifers will read this book to gain encouragement or to strengthen their armor for the battle that is waging in our culture around abortion. I understand that there will also be some Christians who are confused or uninformed on the issue of abortion and have basically remained neutral in the battle. To all of you, we hope to encourage you as you seek a better understanding of the battle we all face.

To be clear, this book is written specifically for those who call themselves followers of Christ, since we are held to a different standard (although all people are welcome to read this book, it is directed at Christians with regard to that standard). As such, I would assume the following of Christ followers:

1. You came to understand that you have a sinful nature that you could do nothing about and stood guilty before a holy, just, and righteous God. In that condition, you would never have been acceptable to God and would have been judged according to your deeds in the flesh,

which the Bible says are tainted by sin and insufficient. In that condition, you would have stood condemned.

2. You heard or read about Jesus, who was God made flesh. Being fully God, He could live a perfect life that was pleasing to God without the taint of sin. Being fully man, He could also identify with human beings and experience the frailty of humanity, be tempted (although He successfully resisted temptation), and be crucified by sinful men. This was done to satisfy the demands of a holy God, who must judge sin (John 3:16). Through the power of God, Jesus was raised from the dead, and by doing so He overcame death.

3. Then God, who is rich in mercy, changed your heart. This is a miraculous work of the Holy Spirit. You *believed* that Jesus died for your sinfulness by paying the price (He took on the burden of God's wrath for you on the cross) that God would otherwise have demanded of you. This is what the Bible calls faith, and it is more than simply mouthing a profession or "walking the aisle." You didn't profess only that you believe that Jesus saved you, but also that you possess faith. This means that you place all of your trust, hope, and commitment in Him.

4. You became an adopted son or daughter of the King of kings and Lord of lords and will spend eternity with Him. Just as Jesus was resurrected, you are promised resurrection after death and a new, glorified body that is incapable of sin.

5. In appreciation for the unspeakable gift of salvation and the promise of eternal life with God, you seek to live a life that pleases Him in every way. Though you will continue to sin, this will not define your life. You seek God's wisdom and guidance through diligent study of His Word and a desire to please Him above all else.

I have presented this brief overview of the gospel to be clear about what I mean when I say "Christian." Jesus says something a bit unnerving in Matthew 7:21–23. He is speaking of the final judgment and says that there will be many who will stand before Him claiming to be His followers, but whose claim He will reject as fraudulent. Where does this deception lie? It would seem that these individuals are professing a claim based on works and not on faith in the person and work of Christ.

In this day, we have many who say they are Christians, but there are tares growing among the wheat in their hearts and lives. We must be believers who are willing to examine ourselves in light of God's Word. Many will say that the Word of God is inconclusive on the subject of abortion. Perhaps someone has tried to convince you that there are passages in the Bible that support abortion. Remember that if you interpret a verse to mean something that is clearly contradicted elsewhere in Scripture, you have misinterpreted the verse. This is referred to as internal authentication. Taking Scripture out of context by not understanding the historical setting or author's intended audience is a common mistake.

The pinnacle of God's creation is humankind. From the first chapter of Genesis, we learn that God created man in His own image. Beginning with the fall of man later in Genesis, the Bible tells us that He values human beings more than all of the rest of His creation. If that is the case, we must be skeptical of any claim that His Word (the Bible) supports the destruction of what He values. There are also some who claim that human beings, while in utero, are not really human beings. Even if you don't believe that Psalm 139 and Jeremiah 1:4–5 reveal God's view of the unborn as human beings, I will address the issue from a scientific standpoint in the chapter titled "When Does Life Begin?"

As the authors, we wish to emphasize that this book is intended to challenge the thinking of Christians. If you take issue with our premise of being nonnegotiable and are not a follower of Jesus Christ, I invite you to get a Bible, find a Bible-believing church, and dig in. It starts but doesn't end with the profession of faith. If you then come to faith and become a believer, we encourage you to read the book and join the conversation.

If you are a true follower of Christ, this book is specifically written for you. While its title may cause you to have questions (good, we got your attention!) or instill within you a resolve to attack the premise, we welcome such a challenge and believe that God's Word is always true—and as such, we must all be subservient to what it has to say to us.

Finally, the title is not considered a litmus test for being a Christian. No, no, a thousand times no! Many non-Christian religions profess to be pro-life or at least speak out against abortion. This in no way qualifies them as Christian or even positions them on the first rung of the ladder to becoming one. Christianity is not a religion of "dos and don'ts" or conservative-versus-liberal viewpoints. You are a Christian by believing the gospel and having faith in Jesus Christ—no more and no less.

When the Holy Spirit changes someone's heart from what the Bible calls a "heart of stone" to a "heart of flesh" (Ezekiel 11:19), that change marks the beginning of a "new creation" (2 Corinthians 5:17) in Christ. This new creation is no longer a slave to sin, but rather is able to discern divine truth. The Bible tells us that a sinful man cannot comprehend this truth and, in fact, sees it as foolishness. This does not mean that a new believer has complete discernment of all truth from the beginning; truth is learned.

There will always be a battle between the old nature, which still remembers the will, mind, and heart that were dominant before the conversion, and the new nature, which is supernaturally implanted by the Holy Spirit. Therefore, in the context of this book, it is possible for a new believer to be confused over the arguments waged between pro-life and pro-choice proponents. If you are a new believer or a believer who has put this issue on the back burner, we wrote this book especially for you. As you grow in your understanding of what God has to say about His creation—specifically what He says about humankind, which He gave the special designation of being created in His image—we hope that it will lead you to a profound understanding of why God considers human life to be so precious.

Is human life inclusive of pre-born humans? That is the pivotal point that clouds this issue for some Christians. This book will attempt to address this point, both scientifically and theologically. In the end, we hope that exploring both of these approaches will help you make an informed decision.

Chapter 1

A YOUNG DOCTOR'S STORY

Dr. Steve Hammond

A young medical resident had just turned 28 years old. He had the world by the tail. The difficult years of medical school were behind him, and he was halfway through his residency and well on his way to realizing his dream of becoming an obstetrician/ gynecologist. He decided to pursue this specialty as soon as he began his obstetrics rotation in medical school. Delivering babies was so interesting to him, and delivering the final product—a squirming, slippery, howling little boy or girl—was always a joyous occasion. It seemed to be a specialty that almost always brought happiness. The long hours were only a minor annoyance at that age because part of the excitement of youth (staying up all night when there was something fun or interesting to do) was still present. He was certain that this was what he wanted to do for the rest of his life.

During his medical school rotation, internship, some moonlighting as an extern, and a year of residency, he had gained experience in both routine and deeply complicated deliveries, in which forceps or breech extractions were required. In addition, he was learning to do Cesarean sections without the presence of a chief resident assistant, along with various gynecological surgeries such as hysterectomies (both abdominal and vaginal) and the newly emerging field of laparoscopy.

Laparoscopy was first developed by gynecologists to perform tubal ligations. Tubal ligation, interruption of the woman's fallopian tubes to accomplish sterilization, had previously been done using a large incision. Laparoscopy allowed this to be done through a small incision in the belly button, making it an outpatient procedure and decreasing cost and recovery time. Today, the expanded use of laparoscopy with videos and special equipment has made it possible to perform major surgeries with small incisions, but during this earlier time laparoscopy was in its infancy. The young doctor had learned to use the laparoscope to do tubal ligations, and it was exciting to be on the cutting edge of this technology.

Laparoscopy was taught during his residency by a physician who oversaw residency training at a Planned Parenthood facility. During this rotation, he was also introduced to a procedure that had just been legalized in the United States four years earlier, the abortion procedure. Again, because of the recent change in the political climate due to the landmark *Roe v. Wade* decision in January 1973 by the Supreme Court of the United States, abortion was now legal, and the young resident saw no reason he shouldn't be a part of this cutting-edge movement. The logic seemed clear to him. Women now had access to legal and "safe" termination of unwanted pregnancies. The arguments were compelling to him, and the expertise to perform the procedure was clearly part of the training that an OB/GYN should receive.

There were some important skills that he had to develop to become good at the procedure. First, he had to be able to determine the approximate gestational age of the fetus by doing a bimanual exam. This involved using a gloved hand in the vagina to push the uterus upward and out of the pelvis so that the other hand could then palpate and determine the size of the uterus. This became important because real-time ultrasound, which can quickly determine gestational age with great accuracy, was not available in 1976. In the early days of abortion, the procedure was performed only during the first trimester (12 weeks and under) in his institution. In fact, the Supreme Court originally intended for only early abortions to be performed (it is only in recent years that late-term abortions have become commonplace in some institutions).

Second, he had to become proficient in dilating the cervix. The cervix is the opening into the womb and is a cylinder that is 2–3 centimeters in diameter and made of firm connective tissue. When labor begins in a full-term pregnancy, the cervix is the part of the anatomy that is examined to determine how much longer the labor is likely to last, and it is measured in centimeters. (Perhaps you have heard the report given to the family in a waiting room: "It won't be long now. . . . The cervix is 9 centimeters dilated!")

During the first trimester of pregnancy, the cervix is closed, and a metal dilator is used to force the cervix open wide enough to insert a plastic cannula (a thin tube). There are other ways to dilate the cervix as well, one of which is to use laminaria (seaweed that is dried out and tightly compressed into a pencil lead-sized roll). It must be inserted into the cervix the day before the scheduled abortion, and by absorbing moisture from the area it swells and slowly forces open the cervix. If the patient cannot make two visits, the dilators must be used. Dilating the cervix can be painful, so a local anesthetic is injected around the cervix. This is called a paracervical block. This step requires some expertise because the cervix can sometimes be tight, and forcing it open can cause lacerations or perforations (in more complex cases).

Once the cervix is dilated, the plastic cannula (6–9 millimeters in diameter) is introduced through the cervix and into the pregnant uterus, another step that requires some expertise. The pregnant uterus is soft, and if care is not taken the cannula can be pushed through the wall of the uterus. This can potentially cause major internal bleeding, and if the perforation is not recognized the cannula can extend into the abdomen. If a cannula is inside the abdomen when suction begins (the next step in the abortion process), it could damage the intestine, bladder, or other vital structures. Knowing how far to insert the cannula and how much pressure to exert on it is a learned skill, and the young doctor was very good at this, too.

Once the suction tubing is connected to the cannula, the abortion officially begins. The opening on the end of the cannula is very small, so it can't remove the fetus intact. First, the amniotic sac (the bag of fluid around the baby) is ruptured. This usually amounts to less than a half-cup of fluid; it's usually clear but becomes bloody as the cannula begins to suction the placenta, membranes, and finally the fetus, which is removed by being torn into pieces. A 6–8-week fetus is only 2 or 3 centimeters long, but even then the pieces of the fetus are recognizable. A 12-week fetus is around 7–10 centimeters long. At this stage, it is easy to recognize fetal parts for what they are: hands, legs, feet, torso, and head (the eyes and mouth are easily discernible). The next step in the process is to collect all of the parts of the fetus and make sure they are all accounted for (away from the view of the woman having the abortion, of course).

Having gained a great deal of experience in performing the procedure, the young doctor largely ignored the crying and occasional pleas to stop the procedure, knowing that this was to be expected and that they were usually past the point of no return when this happened. He learned to dissect the baby parts with the cold clinical approach that a forensic pathologist would employ while doing an autopsy—no emotion. He became so good at this procedure that he was hired by Planned Parenthood to perform abortions for them on Saturdays when he was not on call.

He continued performing abortions at Planned Parenthood for a year—until one Saturday, when he encountered something he had not witnessed before. Saturday procedures were less involved because one of the faculty members interviewed each patient the day prior, took their history, inserted a laminaria, and performed the bimanual exam (presumably the pregnancy term and uterine size were both under 12 weeks). On this particular Saturday, a 16-year-old, who seemed more nervous than the average patient, was the last patient of the morning.

She was a little overweight, so he wasn't suspicious of what was to come. He inserted the cannula just as he had done so many times before, and the amniotic fluid began to flow as usual. Then, more and more of it came, and after a quart or more of fluid, he knew that something was terribly wrong.

Then he felt it. The baby kicked him! The doctor had a one-year-old boy at home, and he knew what a baby's kick felt like. Every time he changed his own little boy's diaper, he experienced the powerful thrust, and this was exactly the same. It didn't stop. He put his hand on her abdomen for the first time, felt the uterus, and confirmed that the baby was squirming violently inside her. She had lied about how far along she was, and the faculty member had missed the fact that she was at least 22–24 weeks pregnant.

A feeling of dread swept over him. What was he going to do now? Eventually, he arranged a transfer to the hospital, and the young girl had to be put to sleep for a D&X (dilation and extraction) completion of what he had started. The baby had to be broken up into small pieces so it could be removed. That was the last abortion he ever did.

I am Dr. Hammond, and that young resident was me.

I was 28 years old at the time. Reflecting now on that time in my life, I was convinced that abortion was just another procedure and that I was helping my patients in the process. I was convinced that if my patient and I decided that the best thing for her was to end her pregnancy, then the government should not interfere. Now, 40 years later, when thinking back on all of the patients I have counseled (often with adverse physical and psychological consequences from a previous abortion), I realize that my conviction at that time had been wrong in so many ways. Clearly, without my involvement many of these abortions would have been done by someone else, but the fact that I have performed more than 700 abortions troubles me to this day.

Speaking with conviction as well as authority, I agree that abortion may seem like a solution in the short term, when there seem to be so many reasons to end a pregnancy and when the prospect of continuing a pregnancy seems so insurmountable. However, I have also learned something significant from the experience of caring for women for more than 40 years, many of whom have shared their stories with me: the painful memories and haunting questions that persist after an abortion take a heavy toll.

I was raised in a Christian home, and from my earliest memories my mother (who was the spiritual leader in my household) taught me about sin and that God had provided a way for me to live forever with Him in heaven. I really had a fairly mature understanding of God as a child. I understood His omnipresence. I felt that He was watching over me, but in my mind that meant that He was "watching me." Nothing I did was outside His sight. I understood this as early as five years of age. I knew that I was not always a "good boy" and that God wasn't pleased with my shenanigans. More than that, I understood that God could not accept me as a part of His family in the condition I was in. At an early age, I would watch Billy Graham on TV and listen intently. I knew that Jesus was my only hope, and I received forgiveness for my sinfulness through a child's faith at an early age.

So what happened? I went from being a young Christian to a physician—well trained in how to care for human beings—who turned his back on his responsibility and ended the lives of more than 700 babies. I could blame the church for not having given me the ammunition to resist the indoctrination I had received in medical school and residency. I could blame my parents for not saying "We raised you better than that" (they didn't say a word against my job of performing abortions). But the truth is that I can only blame myself. I should have been a better student of what the Bible says about the sanctity of human life. I was the one who put those little baby parts back together without flinching after each abortion.

I should have had a new heart that listened to the Holy Spirit and resisted the temptation to perform abortions, much less relish in them. Feeling that baby's kick in the uterus was my wakeup call. It took that incident to bring me to the conclusion that performing an abortion was ending a life, regardless of the gestational age.

Regardless of how you feel about abortion and what I've said so far, let me say that I have been on the other side of this issue and have even *led* the debate on the other side! I have changed my mind and hope to convince you to take another look if you disagree with me. And if you agree with me, I hope to give you courage to become active in the pro-life movement. You can't afford to stand on the sidelines and remain passive any longer.

If you have had an abortion or been personally affected by one, I offer you this reassurance: the Lord Jesus Christ is rich in mercy and will forgive you, no matter what you have done, if you come to Him in repentance and ask Him to forgive you. In John 6:37 Jesus says, "All that the Father gives me will come to me, and whoever comes to me I will never cast out."

He forgave me, and He will forgive you. He is waiting for you to come to Him.

Chapter 2

WHEN DOES LIFE BEGIN?

Dr. Steve Hammond

W hen during the course of a pregnancy does human life begin? Is it immediately after birth? At the point at which the baby could survive outside the womb? At the onset of movement? At implantation? At conception? All of these landmarks during the course of a pregnancy have been proposed.

The Bible has some very clear statements regarding the issue of life before birth, but my focus in this chapter is on science and logic. Since non-Christian critics do not recognize the Bible as authoritative, this chapter is intended to provide information to help you address the audience that you, as a Christian, may have to confront. I hope that the insight provided will make you better equipped to participate in the debate, should the occasion arise.

Clearly, no one would disagree that a squirming, crying newborn is a human being. Whether the baby is full-term or pre-term, he or she is a human being. This raises an interesting point. Whether a baby weighs two pounds or ten pounds, we consider him or her to be a human being. A two-pound baby would only be at 25 weeks' gestation in most cases, which is 15 weeks premature. But if a two-pound baby is born alive, squirming and breathing, he or she is considered a human being, and that baby is protected by law as a human being. If that living baby's life is taken, it is considered murder—the law is clear on that.

The current law of the land in the United States would allow the destruction of a two-pound baby (or any baby at any gestational age) prior to birth, before the first breath. As long as an abortion is performed before the baby is born, it is considered legal. After that, it is not. Technically, there are several phases of the birth process. In a normal vaginal birth, the baby's head first passes through the vagina and is technically outside the woman's body. While no actual breath has been taken by the baby at this point, the baby's face is usually moving, and sometimes the eyes are open and the nostrils are flaring.

I would expect that most people, if polled, would state that this baby is a human being. I raise these points to try to bring into sharp focus the question of whether a baby in the uterus is a human being. By default, our laws say that it is okay to destroy a baby as long as it is inside the womb, before a breath is taken, but not if it is outside the womb.

In this chapter, we are focusing on the point at which a baby is considered a human being. As we consider late-term abortions performed while the baby is still in the womb, it is clear that while it is legal to destroy a baby that can survive outside the womb in the United States today, if one were to state that what is destroyed is not actually a human being, then when does it become human?

I think a rational person would have to agree that nothing apart from time and position (neither of which affects what actually exists) determines when the baby exits the womb. Is this a matter of possession? That is, can a woman say that because the baby resides within her it is her possession to do with as she pleases? If the baby could be considered a human being while residing within the woman's body, then new concerns begin to emerge. Human beings do not give up their right to life depending on their location. This is why it is so important to consider the question of when human life begins. If human life is deemed to exist within the uterus, then the human inside the uterus cannot have her right to life taken away, even if she is located inside another person's body.

So far, we have considered only whether a pre-born baby who is capable of life outside the womb is human. To argue that a two-pound baby inside the womb is not a human being and that the same baby, if outside the womb but moving and breathing, is a human defies common sense and logic. All human beings who reside on this planet were inside a womb at one time. There is no distinction, other than opportunity, between a baby who has been born and another baby at the same age that is still in utero.

Hopefully you are at least considering that human beings exist inside the womb. I was looking through an old family photo album recently, and I found a picture of myself as a five-year-old. I don't look like that young child today, but I am the same human being. So it is with a baby in a mother's womb. All it takes is time and opportunity to transform a baby in utero to a newborn, a five-year-old, or a fully grown adult.

Since there is no biological argument to explain a transformation from inhuman to human, one would have to resort to the legal matter of rights. The argument would be that possession by the mother and the right to do what she wishes with the baby she is carrying supersede any right to life the baby has, and this right is given to the mother by the United States courts. It is clear that courts of law are subject to error, and even the Supreme Court has overturned its own decisions in the past. If there is even the slightest possibility that the baby residing inside a woman is human, shouldn't we err on the side of caution and consider his right to live?

As a practicing physician for more than 40 years, I have a perspective that probably only a few have. Consider my credentials: I aborted more than 700 babies before becoming pro-life, and I inspected their tiny fragmented limbs, heads, and torsos that had been removed during the early stages of pregnancy. I cared for multiple thousands of pregnant women, watching the development of their babies inside them with real-time and 3D ultrasound. I have studied this issue for more than 30 years from a medical, ethical, and religious perspective. I am certainly not infallible, but I reiterate this to make a point regarding the beginning of human life.

All but the most ardent supporters of abortion will agree that a baby who is inside its mother's body just a few seconds before birth is considered a human being. The reasons most would say this are based on logic and experience. After all, what does a woman say after she has a pregnancy loss? She says, "I lost the baby," not "I lost the fetus." This is because the experience of every woman is that if she is pregnant, then she is carrying a baby. Moreover, a moment before birth there is always anticipation. What will she look like? Will he look like the mommy or the daddy? A moment before birth or a moment after birth, a mother or father will consider the baby to be a human being. What, you may be asked, is the difference if the mother and/or father does not want the baby? Does calling it something else change what it is? Sadly, our culture has tried to draw a line of distinction in which a desired fetus equates to a human being but an undesired fetus does not. In reality, no such line exists, but proclamations that it does make the decision to support abortion on demand much easier.

Why, then, do ardent abortion supporters not agree that a moment before birth the baby is not a human being and, therefore, is without rights? The obvious answer is that if the baby has rights, then the high court's decision to allow its destruction is turned upside down and would have to be reconsidered. For this reason alone, you likely will never convince an abortion rights activist to agree that a moment before birth a baby is a human being, but this is an excellent place to start.

I would ask them, "What happens to make the baby a human being at the moment it takes a breath?" This is a question without a clear answer because there is nothing other than the court's arbitrary decision to deem it to be so. Second, if you agree that a baby in the womb is a human being a moment before birth, then when does the fetus-to-human transformation take place? Is there a clear point at which the substance of what is inside the womb changes? Let's look at all the points along the process of intrauterine development to see if we can determine a clear point of demarcation.

The most common point that many abortionists might agree to is that when a baby is viable outside of the womb, they would not support an abortion. After all, they may argue, even if we removed a baby at a certain gestational age, it could not survive outside of the womb on its own. This is a pragmatic and nonscientific answer to the question because viability is not a static point in time.

As a point of reference, my youngest son was born at 26 weeks in 1982. There was little hope that he would survive at that gestational age in 1982, but he beat all the odds and not only survived but is a computer genius today. Due to advances in medicine, the prospect of survival is much greater at 26 weeks today than it was then. Not only is viability dependent on the level of medical expertise to care for the extremely premature infant, but from a medical standpoint viability is also not associated with a dramatic alteration or change in the structure of the baby in utero.

I would argue that the baby didn't go from being nonviable outside the womb on April 22 to being viable on April 23. The viability argument is designed only to placate those who would say that a viable baby should not be destroyed. It does not answer the question of when the baby becomes a human. I would also add that a newborn of any gestational age requires care and nourishment from a parent in order to live. If you take the healthiest full-term baby girl or boy and ignore its needs for food and shelter, it would not survive. Thus, viability outside the womb does not end with birth. Furthermore, neglecting to meet the needs of a newborn can be considered murder by the courts.

Beyond viability, another developmental milestone that some may point to when describing when life begins is the point of quickening, or the mother's recognition of a baby's movement inside her. This is also arbitrary, as some women feel this occur at 14–15 weeks, while others may not feel it until 20–22 weeks or later. Fetal movement is seen on real-time ultrasound as early as 7–8 weeks, so perception by the mother is certainly not the first movement of the baby but only the first perceived movement. Furthermore, movement is only a characteristic of the neuromuscular development of the baby, not a landmark for determining its humanity.

Implantation is another point of development that people may reference. This is the point at which the fertilized egg or zygote burrows into the uterine lining to get nourishment. If implantation does not occur, the fertilized egg will not survive. Indeed, there is not a pregnancy test available that would tell you that a woman was pregnant before implantation, since the pregnancy hormone HCG is not produced in the mother until a few days after this event. Implantation does not change the internal structure of the fertilized egg in any way and, therefore, could not be considered a point of demarcation from inhuman to human.

Since there would not be a positive pregnancy test at this point, no one would seek an abortion at this stage of development regardless. The only reason to debate this point in the first place is in defense of the morning-after pill, which is a high-dose hormone designed to make conditions hostile for the implantation of a fertilized egg. If implantation were the undisputed point of conversion from inhuman to human, then there would be no real objection to its use. However, implantation is only a step along the way, and though it is a necessary step it does not alter the substance of the developing embryo. I would even argue that prevention or disruption of implantation is just as much an abortion as destroying a baby moments before delivery!

The most logical and scientifically defensible answer to the question of when life begins is conception. There are many points to defend this position. First, prior to conception the sperm and the egg have only half the number of chromosomes found in all other human cells. Once they connect, the full complement of chromosomes—23 from the egg and 23 from the sperm—combine to make 46 in the fertilized egg. This new entity is called a zygote, and it is different from all the cells of the mother and father. In fact, except as in the case of identical twins, no other human being who has ever existed on planet Earth has the same chromosomal makeup as this particular zygote.

Uniqueness is only one aspect that differentiates this cell from all other cells of the mother and father; the 46 chromosomes have the ability to direct the development of a new and unique human being from the very moment of conception. While there is usually only one egg produced by a woman each month, the male contributes millions of sperm, but only one of them actually fertilizes the egg. All human beings on this planet were once a single fertilized egg!

I'd also like to discuss the material inside the fertilized egg. I mentioned that there are 46 chromosomes in a fertilized egg, and these chromosomes are arranged in a tightly woven DNA pattern called a double helix. If we could stretch out the chromosomes from a single zygote, the strand would be about two meters long. On each chromosome are units called genes. These genes are like computer code that will determine if the baby is a boy or girl, whether the eyes will be blue or brown, etc. In fact, every characteristic of this eventual adult is embedded in the genetic code on these 46 chromosomes. This is the most incredible computer known to man. If we could take all the genetic material in all the fertilized eggs of all the human beings on planet Earth and compress them together, they would be about the size of two or three aspirin tablets! The genetic material that would be sufficient to replicate the entire human race that is now living on the earth could be encoded in this small amount of genetic material. How incredible!

Once fertilized, the egg begins to divide. First, one cell becomes two cells. Then, something very interesting happens. For a very short time, there are three cells before the three become four. Molecular scientists have determined that as early as this three-cell stage, there is a "communication" between the cells that directs this ultimate differentiation of the zygote into all the cells necessary to create a unique human being. If we were to take a cell from any living animal and stimulate it to replicate itself, it would split, and two would become four, which would then become eight, and so forth.

A skin cell can only divide and produce another skin cell, a liver cell can only produce a liver cell, etc. While so-called stem cells have the ability to make more than one type of cell, no cell has the ability to make all the cells in the body that this now-dividing human zygote has. In vitro fertilization must start with a sperm and an egg. Even cloning, which has been done in animals, requires genetic material from a species and an egg into which the DNA has been injected. Clearly, in the case of people, conception results in a genetically unique zygote that will eventually result in a human being born. Prior to conception, no such potential exists.

If, at conception, a new being with a unique set of chromosomes on which there is unique genetic material is created, we must at least conclude that this new being is genetically separate from the mother who is carrying it. Also, we can conclude that this new being will eventually (if not intentionally or accidentally terminated) become an adult human being.

Although this has been a scientific/philosophical argument, I can't help but reflect on Psalm 139:13–16:

For you formed my inward parts;
>   you knitted me together in my mother's womb
I praise you, for I am fearfully and wonderfully made.
Wonderful are your works;
>   my soul knows it very well.
My frame was not hidden from you,
when I was being made in secret,
>   intricately woven in the depths of the earth.
Your eyes saw my unformed substance;
in your book were written, every one of them,
>   the days that were formed for me,
>   when as yet there was none of them.

King David had not gone to medical school and likely had not even seen a baby delivered. He penned these words not knowing about fertilization/conception, implantation, and fetal development. Nonetheless, he described what I have argued: human life begins at conception. Abortion—the intentional disruption of a pregnancy after conception—is the destruction of a human being.

A MOTHER'S VIEW
ON WHEN LIFE BEGINS

Emily LaBonte

As a mother, I have personal views on life beginning at conception, and as a Christian I can cite biblical evidence/Scripture that points to the same. In doing research for this book, I also have compelling philosophical evidence that points to the same conclusion, and I would like to address that in more detail. While I personally believe strongly that life begins at conception, I want to take a look back at my story before and during the time I was pregnant with my baby girl, Emma Joy.

As newlyweds, my husband, Jon, and I did not know whether we even wanted children. One morning after almost two years of marriage, Jon woke me up, excitedly saying that he'd had a dream. The dream was simple—he saw himself from behind, holding hands with a little girl with light brown, curly hair. He said that in the dream he knew she was our daughter, and her name was Emma Joy. He said that if we ever had a girl, we would have to name her Emma Joy. I agreed because I love the name, but I still thought it would never happen because at the time we did not want children. A few years later, after traveling in Europe, Jon and I came home, and something had changed. The Lord changed our hearts and gave us a desire to have a child.

Looking back, it was amazing to see all the confirmation the Lord was giving us to get pregnant. I am a thin, small-framed, short woman, and multiple people have approached me asking if I was pregnant. I knew I did not look pregnant and was not offended, but I kept wondering why people were asking. One little girl, about two or three years old, even came up to me and asked me directly when I was going to have a baby. . . . I did not even know her! Jon and I just knew that it was time, and after one try I became pregnant with our beautiful Emma Joy.

At first, I wanted a boy, but within just a few weeks of being pregnant I knew my baby was a girl. I immediately forgot about wanting a boy and just wanted her. I cannot explain how I knew, other than by a mother's intuition, and at about 18 weeks it was confirmed that she was indeed a girl. Rewind to 8 weeks of pregnancy; Jon and I heard her heartbeat for the first time, and we both were simply overcome with emotion and cried for joy over the miracle of life!

By 20 weeks (a time when abortion is legal in most states), I began feeling flutters or quickening as my baby was moving inside me! Feeling that for the first time was like magic. It honestly felt like an alien was inside me—it certainly was not my body (a claim that many people use to justify abortion). She continued to grow and get bigger, as did I, and by 26 weeks or so her kicking became violent and even intentional. I love my daughter; she has a bold, spitfire personality, and I knew that would be her temperament, even at 26 weeks of pregnancy. I cannot count the number of times I would be lying on my left side—which was the more comfortable side for me during pregnancy but clearly was not hers—and she would kick me until I rolled over and then immediately settle down. Her personality was so evident, even when she was still in the womb. She is determined to get what she wants, even today!

I believe without a shadow of a doubt that before Jon and I even wanted children, God knew we would have a girl and that she would be called Emma Joy (which means "joy to the world"—something we learned after her birth). God gave that dream to Jon four years before she was born, and now at three years old she indeed is the little girl in his dream—curly, light brown hair and all! God had a plan for her life before we even wanted her, and our initial lack of wanting children had nothing to do with what God had planned for us.

Luke 1:41–44 describes Mary visiting her cousin Elizabeth while they were both pregnant. John the

Baptist leaped for joy in Elizabeth's womb in the presence of the unborn Messiah. The concept of John the Baptist as a fetus leaping for joy—just as my daughter displayed her strong-willed personality in the womb—underscores the fact that babies feel physical stimuli and emotion before they are born. Our personalities, emotions, and ability to feel physical stimuli are all part of our humanity, even in the womb. The womb is simply a location for a baby as it develops, not a magical barrier that keeps a fetus somehow unalive prior to birth.

Consider what Elizabeth—filled with the Holy Spirit, one of the three persons of the one perfect God—says about her own and Mary's unborn children in this passage: "Blessed are you among women, and blessed is the fruit of your womb! And why is this granted to me that the mother of my Lord should come to me? For behold, when the sound of your greeting came to my ears, the baby in my womb leaped for joy" (verses 42–44). Elizabeth is not speaking here; God himself, in the person of the Holy Spirit, is speaking through her. God himself calls an unborn fetus a baby, yet no one questions whether a child or baby is a human life. This is hugely significant! The God of the universe referred to an unborn fetus as life—more specifically, as a baby!

I believe without a doubt that God has a plan for us before conception. God himself spoke to his prophet in Jeremiah 1:5, saying, "Before I formed you in the womb I knew you, and before you were born I consecrated you; I appointed you a prophet to the nations." God knows us and sets us apart before birth; that is what God himself says about His people.

Sermon ends, mic drops.

Just kidding! But, in all seriousness, that is all the evidence I need from the Word to say to my fellow Christians that abortion is wrong. God has a plan for our lives before birth. As Dr. Hammond notes in the previous chapter, David says in Psalm 139:13–14, 16, "For you formed my inward parts; you knitted me together in my mother's womb. I praise you, for I am fearfully and wonderfully made. . . . Your eyes saw my unformed substance; in your book were written, every one of them, the days that were formed for me, when as yet there was none of them." David speaks of the Lord creating and forming him in his mother's womb, with him being fearfully and wonderfully made. No one apart from God himself has the right to destroy what He has made. God takes pride in His creation and He calls us wonderful! Who are we to destroy what He has made?

Scripture is also clear on the fact that God has a plan for each of us before our birth. We should not try to interfere with such a beautiful and sacred thing. Exodus 1:15–22 describes a situation in which the pharaoh of Egypt had ordered the Hebrew midwives to kill Hebrew boys prior to their fully being born. Scripture says that the midwives feared God, so they did not do what Pharaoh asked, . . . and God blessed them. Pharaoh then made a decree to kill the boys after birth. Pharaoh did not see life as sacred, before or after birth, but God does. God blessed the midwives who protected life before and after birth.

In Exodus 21:22–25, God Himself gives Moses instruction for punishing someone who inflicts injury on a pregnant woman, causing the child to come out. God allowed a fine if no harm had been done. However, if harm had been done, God said to take life for life (an eye for an eye). Many scholars believe that this law was citing an instance in which a pregnant woman suffered a permanent injury related to her ability to have children (i.e., infertility from the injury), and/or her unborn child potentially suffered a permanent injury. This law would have required waiting until the woman gave birth to know whether any such injury had occurred, whether it was harm to her fertility or to her unborn child. Even if no injury had occurred, the man who had hit the pregnant woman was still penalized due to the anxiety caused for the pregnant woman and her husband in facing a possible injury, which was determined by the court and the woman's husband. If someone were injured permanently— whether it was the woman, the child, or both—the penalty had to match the severity of the damage. This was the Bible's first talion law, a law that ensured that a penalty matched the severity of the injury imposed.[4]

I believe that God made it a point to specify a pregnant woman (not just any woman) in this instance, and He also to refer to what comes out of the woman as a child. If the injury or loss of life referred to the woman alone, the text could have made a generalization and simply referred to the woman, but there is a reason it does not. God values the life of an unborn fetus just as much as He values the life of an adult. All of these examples refer to life beginning at conception, which is prior to birth. God counted us worthy for Him to send His Son to die for us. He loves us, and we should do a better job of loving each other, especially in this context of the unborn.

If you still aren't convinced about the sanctity of life, Matthew 5:21–22 reveals how murder—and even the potential of murder—is sin. Scripture says that we are subject to judgment or even hell if we are angry with or speak ill of a brother or sister. That is because the Lord judges not only our actions but also our thoughts, which can and many times do lead to actions. An unkind thought or word may not seem like murder in our eyes, but it is in God's eyes because the sin has been committed in our hearts. Likewise, based on Scripture's explanation of God's view of life, a zygote (or fertilized egg) may not look like life as we understand it, but it is indeed life in God's eyes.

So far, we have discussed the question of when life begins scientifically (in the previous chapter), experientially, and biblically. I now want to address the question philosophically and explore why our legal system cannot define when life begins.

First, I would like you to ask yourself what the difference is between a woman aborting a 32-week fetus, someone other than the mother killing a 32-week fetus, and someone murdering a newborn infant who is born prematurely at 32 weeks (which no one would dispute is murder). The differences have to do with which person is killing the child and the location of the child (inside or outside the womb). Are these differences substantial enough to justify abortion?

In doing research for this book, I came across a persuasive philosophical argument for why fetuses in utero are indeed alive. Stephen Schwartz presented the acronym SLED (size, level of development, environment, and degree of dependency) to debunk abortion advocates' persuasions,[5] and I would like to go through each of his points.

Let's first address the difference of size. Does your size determine your humanity? My personal answer is no—my daughter is no less human as a 25-pound two-year-old than she will be as an adult weighing more than 100 pounds within the next couple of decades. Likewise, a 32-week unborn fetus at four pounds is no less human than a day-old infant born at eight pounds.

In fact, the 32-week fetus, if given the opportunity to be born (though extremely small in size), would likely scream just like the eight-pound infant born one day earlier. It would have a heartbeat, breathe, eat, grow, and go through every other function a normal child would. In fact, a 32-week fetus on a real-time ultrasound has all of the same body parts and looks just like a miniature version of a full-term newborn because that is exactly what she is—a miniature human, still inside her mother's uterus. Comparing a two-year-old toddler's size to that of an adult, though there is a significant difference between the two, does not make the two-year-old any less human than the adult. If you agree that this is true and are a pro-abortion believer, please consider that a four-pound fetus is no less human than an eight-pound, day-old infant because of its small size.

The next difference I want to address is the level of development. Is a teenager more human than a toddler because she/he has developed higher cognitive skills and the ability to drive a car? Certainly not; they are simply at different stages of life. If that is true, then is an 18-week-old fetus that already has ears, genitals, a beating heart, and flexing muscles that can be seen on an ultrasound (and that is also legal to abort in any of the United states) any less human than a day-old newborn? I would argue that it is definitely not. The only differences are the amount of time the child has been given to develop and the fact that the newborn has taken his first breath. Pro-abortion advocates would have you believe that a baby does not become human until she takes her first breath. While there may be something emotionally magical for parents when their child takes that first breath, there is nothing scientific or biblical that would support that the first breath defines the beginning of humanity; that occurs much earlier (I would argue at conception).

Next, does the environment make a difference in our humanity? Does being outside a building make one person more human than someone else inside a building? Further, is it okay for a man to shoot another man dead inside a building versus outside? That seems ridiculous to ask, right? However, when applied to a fetus inside the womb, legally there is a difference. Due to location alone, the fetus is deemed nonhuman and has no rights simply due to the fact that he/she is still in the mother's uterus, albeit a totally separate entity from the mother. In some states, even if the little human could survive without life support, it is still legal to destroy her with abortion simply because she has not been born yet. Does being inside its mother make a child less human than a child outside its mother? I would argue that it does not.

Finally, does one's degree or lack of dependency determine their humanity? In other words, does dependence upon another person or thing determine who you are? Is someone on dialysis less human because they depend on a machine to survive compared to someone with normal kidney function? Absolutely not. If that is the case, is a pre-term fetus (or · zygote, for that matter) any less human just because he depends on his mother for survival? If given time and nourishment, the child would likely be born a healthy, screaming infant within a few months. For that matter, a newborn is highly dependent on his parents for survival as well, but is still given the same rights for life as an adult—as it should be. The newborn cannot live without nourishment and care from his parents, but that does not determine his humanity, just as it should not determine the humanity of an unborn child.

The legal system is trying to define when life begins but is contradicting itself in many ways. Let me explain.

There are inconsistencies with our laws everywhere. It is legal to abort fetuses up to 20 weeks of gestation or the point of viability (which is determined by the physician) in all states; some states have no limitation at all on when an abortion can be performed.[6] Now, let's compare that information with some contradicting laws. According to the United States Children's Bureau, 14 states and the District of Columbia include prenatal drug exposure in their definition of child abuse and · neglect.[7] This means that it is legal to abort and destroy a fetus but is considered illegal and child abuse if the

mother uses drugs during pregnancy. According to
Cornell Law School (article 18 U.S. Code § 3596 —
Implementation of a sentence of death), it is a federal
law that a death sentence cannot be carried out on
a pregnant woman.[8] This is interesting to me, to say
the least; a woman can abort her unwanted fetus by
decision, but the fetus of a pregnant felon on death row
is given the opportunity to live.

According to the National Conference of State
Legislatures, 38 states currently have fetal homicide
laws, criminalizing acts that harm a fetus by anyone
other than the mother.[9] In basic terms, this means that
if a woman decides to have an abortion, it is okay to
destroy the fetus, but if a fetus is killed by someone
other than the mother through abortion, it is illegal.
Do you see the inconsistencies?

Does it surprise you that sex-selective abortion
(abortion performed based on the predicted sex of the
child) occurs frequently in other countries because of
the perceived higher value of having a male child over
a female child? Does it surprise you that pro-choice
organizations here in the United States are against
making this kind of practice illegal because they say
it will create obstacles to women's healthcare?[10] In
essence, they are saying that women should be able to
choose to abort based on sex alone because screening
for women wanting to abort based on sex alone would
cause a delay for a woman seeking abortion and, in

return, would harm women's access to healthcare. This is totally bogus to me!

Pro-abortion advocates want to make access to abortion as easy as buying a tube of toothpaste; they do not want women to have time to change their minds or even think about their decision before it is done. They are completely dehumanizing the unborn fetus for the sake of "women's health." Just because something is legal does not mean that it is moral.

Consider historical situations like Nazi Germany or the practice of slavery in the U.S. until 1865. It was legal for Germans to experiment on and brutally kill Jews during the Holocaust simply because of their race, and it was legal in the United States to own another human being based on skin color until slavery was made illegal in 1865. As we know now, it is immoral to kill someone based on their race or to own another human being.

We do not need the legal system to tell us these things in order for us to realize that they are wrong, but, unfortunately, legality does shape public opinion a great deal, regardless of the morality or immorality. We should not go to the legal system to determine our values; we should look to the author of our values, the Creator of the universe. He is our judge, and we will reap the consequences of our sin, whether the act is legal or not.

Galatians 6:7 says, "Do not be deceived: God is not mocked, for whatever one sows, that will he also reap." Do not be deceived—if you are a woman trying to escape the consequences of sinful actions (i.e., an unwanted baby) by destroying that unborn child, you will reap what you have sown. Our God is so gracious and loving, but He also promises consequences for our sinful actions and disciplines those He loves. The legal system is in place to help guide and protect us, but we must also be prudent as believers to compare the written laws of our legal system to the Word of God. I would even go so far as to say that we should disobey the law of the land if it is against God's commands. Acts 5:29 says that we must obey God rather than men.

I believe that the greatest genocide of history is currently taking place. According to the Guttmacher Institute, approximately 926,200 abortions were performed in our country in 2014, and some 1.5 percent of women ages 15–44 had an abortion.[11] Close to one million abortions occur yearly in the United States, then, and it is legal for this to continue under current laws—but I do not believe it is morally right.

I will leave you with one more thought to consider: for those who say that a fetus is not a life, why is it difficult to watch a video such as *The Silent Scream* by Bernard Nathanson[12] or see pictures of aborted fetal body parts? I have heard pro-abortion advocates describe pictures of aborted fetuses as propaganda that is used to rouse emotions. I even had a pro-abortion acquaintance actually say a curse over my family for sending him a link to *The Silent Scream*.

Why? Because truth can be offensive and painful, especially if you do not hold that truth or live your life by it! We are a prideful creation, and we hate it when we are wrong. Yes, *The Silent Scream* and pictures of aborted fetuses stir the emotions of anyone I have ever known to look at them, but they are not propaganda. It is true that it is absolutely sickening to see a tiny human mutilated into small bits, but what is seen is truly what is being done. Some evidence now shows that an unborn baby feels pain by 20 weeks and suffers when an abortion is performed. An act based on that evidence—called the Pain-Capable Unborn Child Protection Act—passed in the House in October 2017 for the third time but still has not passed in the Senate.[13]

My hope for you is this: if seeing these things causes you to question the humanity of these little ones in any way, please stop for a moment, drop your pride, consider that you may be wrong (we all make mistakes), and ask yourself whether they are indeed humans who deserve the right to live. Your belief may make the difference in a life—if not in the lives of many.

Chapter 4

HOW DOES GOD VIEW ABORTION?

Dr. Steve Hammond

An American man serving in Europe during World War II brought home a Nazi soldier's helmet with "*Gott Mit Uns*" (God with us) inscribed on the inside. It is easy to conclude that the owner of the helmet was tragically in error, knowing what we now know about the Holocaust. But do we sometimes make the same mistake? We sing "God Bless America"—a plea for God's blessings upon our country—but do we ever ask how we (Christians) should bless God? The question is not "Is God on our side?" but rather, "Are we on God's side?"

We have tried to filter the information in this book through the lens of God's Word; the God-given heart of a Christian wife and mother; and the experience of a Christian physician who, once an abortionist, has since changed his mind. We have prayed that God would guide us in what we wrote on these pages so that these words would bring honor to Him.

Let me now use a philosophical approach to try to answer the question posed in the title of this chapter: How does God view abortion? When you cut to the chase, there are only three possible answers: pro-life, pro-abortion (meaning He might favor the opinion that says it is okay for a woman to abort her unborn child), or neutral on the issue. Let's expand upon all three of these potential answers.

First, let's assume that the premise of this book is correct and that God, who creates all life, supports the preservation of life and is opposed to all methods of abortion, whether they be chemical or surgical. As I read the Bible and try to understand God's position on moral issues, I am convicted that He never takes a tolerant position on sin. He is quite dogmatic about it, in fact, and in many places He tells us that whatever is not in line with His truth is sin.

In this scenario, God would not be a proponent of life and yet lenient on abortion—therefore, we can conclude from all of the biblical evidence that all abortion is sin. (If you believe there are options that would predispose God otherwise, consult the neutrality option later in this chapter.) If God is pro-life, He will judge the hearts of all who support abortion, whether they are Christian or non-Christian. Now, the sin of the Christian is covered by the blood of Christ, as is all sin. However, the Christian who knows the truth and persistently violates his conscience is disobedient and will have to answer for that. In summary, if God is pro-life, He will consider all other views on this subject to be sin.

Second, let's assume that God is pro-abortion. Though we believe that the Word of God contradicts this premise, we would ask the Christian who would support this premise to point to Scripture that would allow one to come to this conclusion. There are numerous passages that either state directly or imply by direct inference that God is the Creator and sustainer of life and that, by virtue of that alone, He would oppose the termination of innocent life.

One of the ways in which we interpret Scripture is called internal corroboration. This means that if a single verse is hard to explain, and if it could mean one of two things that are in direct contradiction with one another, but several other Scripture references clearly indicate that one of them is correct, then it is safe to conclude that the correct interpretation of the verse in question is that which aligns with other scriptural references.

No single verse or idea in the Bible could overcome the plethora of verses that indicate God's opinion of life. In Leviticus 18–20 a collection of abominations is listed and highlighted in reference to the Canaanite god Molech and the practice of child sacrifice. Israelites were to have no part of this pagan practice. Though this is a reference to a pagan god, and the idea of throwing a living child into a furnace and burning them alive is abhorrent to all of us, shouldn't the sacrifice of the unborn to the god of convenience be similarly abhorrent? This certainly paints a picture of God's opinion of destroying innocent human life. The antithesis of the destruction of life is the loving protection of life. It is clear that God loves human beings. This is mentioned so many times that we need not highlight any other verse than John 3:16, which is very likely the first verse we learned as children.

Wasn't the following the first song you learned in Sunday School as a child?

> Jesus loves me, this I know
> For the Bible tells me so.
> Little ones to Him belong
> They are weak, but He is strong.
>
> Yes, Jesus loves me!
> Yes, Jesus loves me!
> Yes, Jesus loves me!
> The Bible tells me so.

Finally, let's assume that God is neutral on the subject of abortion or that abortion can be justified on the basis of any of the common reasons that are given: rape, incest, or fetal malformation. We are not, by any means, saying that these circumstances are not difficult moral dilemmas. But God is sovereign. He doesn't make mistakes. Though it is so difficult on this side of eternity to see how He works everything out for our eventual good (Romans 8:28), we can rest assured that He does.

Remember, we aren't in charge of making decisions for unbelievers. When unbelievers are faced with this kind of difficulty, the situation is our opportunity to love them, support them, and share the gospel if the opportunity presents itself. Tragedy is the most fertile ground for evangelism. Rape and incest are the only situations in which the law allows an innocent victim to be given the death penalty while the perpetrator either goes free or serves only minimal jail time. The US Department of Justice says the following:

> "While the average sentence of convicted rapists released from state prisons has remained stable at about 10 years, the average time served has increased from about 3-1/2 years to about 5 years; for those released after serving time for sexual assault, the sentence has been a stable 6-1/2 years, and the average time served grew about 6 months to just under 3 years."[14]

As you can see, one of the victims who has had nothing to do with the atrocity (the unborn) is put to death, and the other victim (the mother) is given little justice for what she has been forced to endure. Again, we are not trying to minimize a terrible crime or encourage any woman to do so. We are simply trying to imagine how God might respond to a believer if she prayed: "God, what is your will for me in this situation?"

For the unbeliever faced with difficult circumstances, this again may present an opportunity for evangelism. What we are trying to convey is that while we can have opinions on difficult situations like these, we need not be inflexible. When asked for an opinion regarding rape and incest, the believer can say, "For me, the question is easier than it is for the unbeliever. I value life, and while it would be difficult for me to apply this principle personally, I could have the child, and if I couldn't bear raising it, I would give it up for adoption." This is not a trite response on my part (Dr. Hammond). My daughter gave me this answer when she was 18 years old!

We often hear voiced an exception regarding the health or life of the mother. The truth is that the life of the mother in today's medicine is almost never an issue. An ectopic pregnancy, in which the pregnancy implants outside the uterus, is not a consideration. This extrauterine pregnancy can sometimes be advanced to the point that a fetal pole and fetal heartbeat can be seen. Unfortunately, when the pregnancy is implanted outside the womb, there is no choice other than sacrificing the pregnancy; otherwise, there could be a catastrophic rupture of the tube that could lead to hemorrhage and maternal death. No one disputes this indication for pregnancy interruption; there is no way to remove and implant the pregnancy in the proper place. The choice not to intervene and remove the ectopic pregnancy always results in eventual pregnancy loss and potentially risks the mother's life as well.

This is not a choice between the mother or the fetus. The fetus cannot survive to viability in the ectopic location, and lack of intervention risks the life of the mother as well. The life of the mother can also be at stake when preeclampsia (a condition that can result in a medical emergency that usually reverses when the baby and placenta are removed) occurs in the second trimester before viability. In some circumstances, the baby must be delivered prematurely by necessity. Even though the baby may not be viable, the idea is not to destroy the baby but to remove the pregnancy to reverse the medical emergency caused by preeclampsia.

There are certain cardiovascular (heart) conditions of the mother that can be exacerbated if she becomes pregnant. In my 35 years of practicing obstetrics, only one mother out of more than 25,000 for which my group provided care had such a condition. The patient had Eisenmenger's complex, which is a congenital heart defect that is particularly dangerous for women as they progress further along in pregnancy. Labor and delivery—with all of the pushing and sudden shift in blood volume—can be catastrophic. This particular patient elected to carry her pregnancy in spite of the risk to her own life, and she delivered a healthy baby.

Although she later had a heart transplant, she and her baby both survived.

The point is that a woman at term with a condition that requires the baby to be destroyed to preserve the mother's life never occurs. Either the problem is discovered early in pregnancy, when proper care and available options can be offered, or the baby is immature (as in the rare case of preeclampsia prior to viability, as mentioned above), where preterm delivery is unavoidable. Another issue is in the rare event that cancer is discovered while a woman is pregnant. The most common cancer is breast cancer, which occurs around one in 3,000 pregnancies. Depending on the stage and grade of tumor, surgery can be performed and even some chemotherapy administered, if necessary, after the first 12 weeks of pregnancy without harm to the preborn baby. This doesn't affect the long-term survival of the mother.[15] Terminating the pregnancy does not improve survival of the mother. In fact, one study showed that women who aborted their babies in hopes of obtaining faster and better treatment actually had shorter survival rates than those women who carried their babies to term.[16]

The health of the mother is another issue altogether. Performing an abortion to preserve the health of the mother is a commonly used rationale to justify the need for abortion. The implication is that the pregnant woman will be healthier if she has an abortion than if she carries and delivers the baby.

Health can be physical or mental, and I would argue that except in rare circumstances physical health is not the issue. The one who decides that a pregnant woman would be healthier if an abortion were performed is the abortionist. Using health of the mother as an excuse is an attempt to justify a decision of convenience with a respectable label. The claim is often that the woman's mental health would be undermined if an abortion were not performed. This determination is questionable at best, given that regret and remorse plague most women who terminate pregnancies—often for years.

God is never neutral on moral issues. His Word draws clear lines of distinction between right and wrong. In the book of Revelation, John delivers a message to the church at Laodicea based on his objection to their being lukewarm. "I know your works: you are neither cold nor hot. Would that you were either cold or hot! So, because you are lukewarm, and neither hot nor cold, I will spit you out of my mouth" (Revelation 3:15–16). They knew the truth but lived lives that compromised that truth.

Could God, who makes emphatic statements in passages such as Psalm 139 and Jeremiah 4, imply that doing what is right is dependent on human preference? Clearly, God does not support moral neutrality. Think about this before you try to approach abortion from a perspective of neutrality. If you say that you don't believe in abortion but do support another woman's right to have one, aren't you trying to avoid taking a position by being neutral? However, we must remember that our conviction that abortion is wrong does not mean that we can sit on the sidelines and point a finger of condemnation. In fact, pro-life Christians may be rightly condemned for pointing accusing fingers at abortion and its victims without offering comfort to the victims themselves, providing loving advice for those truly seeking answers, and helping those who are in desperate situations.

SANCTITY OF LIFE AND RELATED TOPICS

Emily LaBonte

n this chapter, I want to discuss a few related topics: the sanctity (holiness/sacredness) of human life, rights, and the choice of abortion versus life. I first want to talk about how God sees human life: He sees it as precious, worth protecting, and even worth dying for. Then I will dive into the many issues surrounding choice, rights, and the terms *pro-choice*, *pro-abortion*, and *pro-life*.

In Genesis 1:26, Father God says to Jesus and the Holy Spirit, "Let us make man in our image, after our likeness. And let them have dominion over the fish of the sea and over the birds of the heavens and over the livestock and over all the earth and over every creeping thing that creeps on the earth." The next verse says, "So God created man in his own image, in the image of God he created him; male and female he created them." The God of the universe created humans—but no other created thing—in His likeness! He sets us apart from any other earthly creation by creating us to bear His image. In our very creation, He made the human race sacred, set apart above all else. In Psalm 8:5–6, David says,

> When I look at your heavens, the work of your
>   fingers,
>   the moon and the stars, which you have set
>   in place,
> what is man that you are mindful of him,
>   and the son of man that you care for him?
>
> Yet you have made him a little lower than the
>   heavenly beings
>   and crowned him with glory and honor.
> You have given him dominion over the works
>   of your hands;
>   you have put all things under his feet.

David starts out by asking God a question: What are human beings compared to the wonders of the heavens? He then answers the question: humans are above everything else on earth, just below the angels of heaven! In Leviticus 18–20, God Himself warns the people of Israel not to sacrifice their children. God says that child sacrifice profanes the name of God. One can only wonder: Is abortion modern-day child sacrifice? Abortion is sacrificing a living, pre-born child at the altar of convenience (in the great majority of cases).

Some fetuses are aborted because of birth defects and even gender selection. Humans may call a child with a birth defect not worthy of saving, but that child has indeed been fearfully and wonderfully made by the Creator of the universe in His own image. God created us in His image, set us above any other creation on earth, made us rulers of His creation, and then sent His son to die for us because He counted us worthy and charged us to love one another. First John 4:10, 12 says, "In this is love, not that we have loved God but that he loved us and sent his Son to be the propitiation for our sins. . . . Beloved, if God so loved us, we also ought to love one another. No one has ever seen God; if we love one another, God abides in us and His love is perfected in us."

Let this sink in: If God counts us worth dying for, please consider that this applies to the unborn as well. God loves them so much, as He does the rest of humankind, that He sent His Son to die for them. We must love the unborn as God loves the unborn. In Jeremiah 1:5 God says to His prophet, "Before I formed you in the womb I knew you, and before you were born I consecrated you; I appointed you a prophet to the nations." God knows us, too, and sets each of us apart before birth; I believe this proves His love for us even before our birth. However, He calls us to love one another as well. In Matthew 22:37–39, Jesus says, "You shall love the Lord your God with all your heart and with all your soul and with all your mind. This is the great and first commandment. And a second is like it: You shall love your neighbor as yourself."

I believe the unborn are our neighbors; I also believe that they are severely oppressed because they have no voice. Let us love these little neighbors by speaking on their behalf; let us speak against the injustice of abortion. Let us place their lives in the hands of God—the only rightful judge to determine whether they live or die.

The Bible values the poor, oppressed, and widowed. In Jeremiah 22:3, the Lord says, "Do justice and righteousness, and deliver from the hand of the oppressor him who has been robbed. And do no wrong or violence to the resident alien, the fatherless, and the widow, nor shed innocent blood in this place."

In James 2:15–16, James says, "If a brother or sister is poorly clothed and lacking in daily food, and one of you says to them, 'Go in peace, be warmed and filled,' without giving them the things needed for the body, what good is that?" The Bible clearly calls us to take care of those less fortunate by taking action. We should not only never do wrong to others or shed innocent blood but also should actively do what is right and beneficial on their behalf.

The Bible also talks about the taking of life, explicitly stating that God alone has the rightful place to take a life. One of the Ten Commandments instructs us not to murder. In Deuteronomy 32:39, Moses describes God as stating, "See now that I, even I, am he, and there is no god beside me; I kill and I make alive; I wound and I heal; and there is none that can deliver out of my hand." Because the Lord has sanctified us, we should love one another, including the unborn, and realize that it is God's right, and His alone, to kill.

God revealed an attribute of Himself through Moses as the one who kills and makes alive. He explicitly says that there is no god aside from Him; we should not play God by taking the life of an unborn person—only God has the right to choose who lives or dies. If you find yourself wondering about the point when life begins, please reference the chapter titled "When Does Life Begin?"

The argument that women have rights to their own bodies is a key area of contention among those who advocate for abortion. Somehow abortion has been twisted to fall in line with women's rights issues— similar to women receiving equal pay as men, getting the types of jobs they want, having the right to vote, etc. In her book, Mara Hvistendahl details much of French demographer Christophe Guilmoto's work. Guilmoto has determined that 160 million females are missing in the world, with sex-selective abortion having played a large role as males are favored over females in many cultures, especially in Asia. The overabundance of men in parts of the world has even led to threats against women, including bride buying, sex trafficking, and forced marriages.[17] If abortion were universally considered a global women's rights issue, I would not think that sex-selective abortion— where one sex is favored over another—would be an occurrence. This is a contradiction.

In pregnancy, a woman's body changes dramatically. Her abdomen becomes very large in most cases, and the woman may develop swelling in her legs and experience significant discomfort due to having another human growing inside her. In rare cases, a woman's body may become traumatized, as in cases of peripartum cardiomyopathy, where pregnancy places long-term strain on the heart. In even rarer cases, a mother may die from the stress on her body from pregnancy and the delivery of the baby. This is not something that I, personally, take lightly. There is certainly a risk involved in becoming pregnant.

However, this risk is extraordinarily low and can never be predicted. Specifically, peripartum cardiomyopathy affects previously healthy pregnant women with a low incidence of 0.1 percent of pregnancies,[18] and pregnancy-related mortality had an incidence of less than 0.02 percent in 2013.[19] Compare this with the nearly 1 million abortions performed yearly in the United States. Also, it is my belief that people must accept responsibility for and the consequences of their actions. In the case of engaging in sex, people should live with and accept the potential consequence of pregnancy and, in return, do the best thing for the unborn child—whether it is carrying, delivering, and keeping the child or placing the child for adoption.

While there may be life-threatening risks involved for some pregnant women, for those who choose to have abortions it is important to remember that the decision does not just impact the mother's body, but that of another human being as well. During late-term abortion, the baby's skull is crushed so that it can be more easily removed. It is known that the rights of some are protected by restrictions on the freedoms of others, so giving rights to the unborn would most definitely restrict those of women getting abortions. The truth is that not everyone can have their way because worldviews and laws around individual freedoms may clash.

In this case, there are no laws enforced to protect the unborn victims; they have no rights. In no other circumstance is it legal to destroy another human life—abortion is the only legal way to kill another human except in war and in states where the death penalty is enforced. Why? In most cases, when a woman undergoes an abortion she is trying to stop the changes that will occur to her body in pregnancy that were described above and any inconvenience that might result from the birth of a child, including the financial responsibilities that come with bringing that life into the world. She may even go as far as to believe that the child would be better off not being born than to have a mother who can't support her. However, she is taking another life when she does this—the most defenseless type of life that cannot speak for itself. Women need to understand that they are not just removing a blob of tissue or terminating a pregnancy; they are terminating the life of an unborn human baby.

Many women say that they have the right to do whatever they want with their bodies. As a believer, I gave up the right to my own body when I started diving deeper into the Word and realized that I do not have rights to my body. Take Romans 12:1–2, for instance, which says,

> I appeal to you therefore, brothers, by the mercies of God, to present your bodies as a living sacrifice, holy and acceptable to God, which is your spiritual worship. Do not be conformed to this world, but be transformed by the renewal of your mind, that by testing you may discern what is the will of God, what is good and acceptable and perfect.

In 2 Corinthians 4:8–10 Paul says, "We are afflicted in every way, but not crushed; perplexed, but not driven to despair; persecuted, but not forsaken; struck down, but not destroyed; always carrying in the body the death of Jesus, so that the life of Jesus may also be manifested in our bodies."

As believers, our bodies are not our own, and we should not claim possession of them. "Or do you not know that your body is a temple of the Holy Spirit within you, whom you have from God? You are not your own, for you were bought with a price. So glorify God in your body," states the apostle in 1 Corinthians 6:19–20.

The Lord deserves for us to sacrifice any right we may claim to our bodies so that He may do whatever He desires with them—our hands, our feet, our minds, our hearts, our choices, and so forth. If you are a believer; have fallen short of the glory of God, as we all have (Romans 3:23); experience an unwanted/unintended pregnancy inside or outside a biblical marriage; and do not know your next step, then I encourage you to offer your body to the Lord. Fervently seek His will for your life. I can promise that it does not start with ending the life inside you.

Dear brothers and sisters, there are consequences for our actions, and I know this firsthand. I personally had an unintended/unwanted pregnancy in my college years before I met my husband. When I finally accepted that I was going to be a mother, I lost the baby when I was two months pregnant. The Lord did not intend for me to be a mother at that time, and I have made peace with that; He alone has the right to give and to take away. He wanted my heart and my obedience, and through that situation and the loss of a child He has gained my obedience, as He has my heart. I am not my own; my body is an empty vessel for the Lord to use as He wills. He is relentless in His pursuit of our hearts—praise God! Rest assured, God will do so much more with your temple if you allow Him than you could ever do based on your own will.

Now, I'd like to take a look at what *pro-choice* actually means. From the founding of our country to where we are today, the Declaration of Independence has proclaimed that we all have unalienable rights of life, liberty, and the pursuit of happiness that were given to us not by government, but by our Creator. The government's job was never to create these rights but to protect them. In essence, everyone is "pro-choice."

Even so, I believe that the term *pro-choice* is deceptive; it is propaganda formed by pro-abortion advocates and intended to rest easier on the ears than the term *pro-abortion*, which sounds too close to "pro-death" or "pro-killing." If we break down the actual definition, the term means that any person can choose whether or not abortion is acceptable; any woman can decide for herself whether or not to abort her unborn child.

The term even extends to those who may not agree with abortion personally but do not want to push their beliefs onto others, even if they believe the decision to abort to be wrong or evil. People especially do not want to push their views on other women in the cases of rape or incest because the circumstances are so horrific and unrelatable for many.

What they do not realize or choose to ignore is the fact that instances of women seeking abortions after rape are extraordinarily rare. Specifically, the Guttmacher Institute released a research article in 2005 revealing that 1 percent of women out of a sample size of 1,160 had an abortion due to having been a victim of rape in 2004, and 1 percent of women out of a sample size of 1,900 chose abortion due to having been a victim of rape in 1987. The rate of pregnancy from incest was less than 0.5 percent in both population sets. The majority of women who had abortions cited the following reasons: having a baby would dramatically change their life; they couldn't afford a baby; they didn't want to be a single mother; or they were having relationship problems.[20]

Most women get abortions for the sake of convenience, not because their life is threatened or they fear seeing their rapist's face in the eyes of their child. When people identify as pro-choice and vote in such a manner, it is legalized for any woman to have an abortion—killing the unborn child, even if it is wrong or evil to do so—because not enough people are speaking up to say that aborting an unborn human being is wrong. Now that many have decided to live in this gray area, abortion is legal up to the point of viability in all states. If one votes pro-choice, that person is actually voting pro-abortion because the choice that is being forced is abortion, not the choice of life. There is no law protecting the unborn from abortion for the sake of convenience in any state. On average, the lives of approximately 1 million unborn fetuses are terminated every year in the United States alone. Not all choices are right; there is no gray zone in this matter. There is pro-life or pro-abortion—both are choices.

There are also cases in which women do not get a choice at all. While some pro-abortion advocates would make the availability of abortion as easy as buying toothpaste, this would make it very difficult to obtain thorough and informed consent, screen for any coercion factors, or give a mother the time to think through her decision entirely. I would argue that this is not pro-choice at all. In fact, if it were, wouldn't pro-choice advocates want women to be totally informed about their choice, making sure that they are not being forced to have an abortion against their will and giving them time to become educated about all of the alternatives, such as adoption?

By trying to abolish 24-hour waiting periods for the sake of eliminating barriers for women to get access to healthcare, pro-choice advocates are eliminating the choice component entirely, as it is very difficult to be totally informed and think through such a large decision without some sort of waiting period. Believe it or not, when women are given a waiting period, many choose not to have an abortion and end up birthing beautiful, healthy children they either keep or put up for adoption.

With a waiting period, women have an opportunity to change their minds on a potentially life-altering decision. According to one study, 2 percent of women from Utah who planned to have abortions (out of a sample of 500) changed their minds and chose to have their babies instead.[21] While this may not be statistically significant, I can only imagine that the ten babies who were given an opportunity to live would beg to differ. If it were saving even one life, I would say it would be worth it!

Bernard Nathanson, a former abortionist and one of the leading figures in getting *Roe v. Wade* passed, also changed his mind. He admittedly inflated maternal death statistics in order to help pro-abortion legislation pass and continue his lucrative abortion endeavors.[22] My wonderful co-author of this book, Dr. Hammond, changed his mind as well. Dr. Hammond recently shared an email with me from the pro-life association for obstetricians and gynecologists. The email concluded with the information that the World Medical Association is trying to pass an ethics policy that requires doctors to refer for abortion, even against their conscience.

While the World Medical Association has no legal jurisdiction in any country, this organization highly influences future legislation around the world.[23] That is a scary thought: pro-life OB/GYNs could be forced to refer patients for abortion, even against their own beliefs! How is this pro-choice? Pro-abortion advocates are also minimizing the gravity of the abortion procedure altogether; they want women to think that a potentially life-altering decision is no big deal at all—that there are no consequences aside from making a problem go away.

In many states, teenagers are not even required to inform their parents before an abortion procedure,[24] so a 13-year-old can have an abortion without telling her mom or dad. Many would argue that a teenager is not developed enough to make such a large decision or think through the options logically. Again, the term *pro-choice* is just propaganda; the choice is literally life or death.

I have heard it said that providing options, including abortion, increases the likelihood that women will learn about alternatives. Advocates also say that if abortion is legal abortion rates will decrease, and if abortion is illegal women will resort to taking matters into their own hands by any means necessary, thus increasing maternal death rates. Studies have revealed otherwise; one Danish study in particular revealed that "increased risks of death were

45 percent, 114 percent, and 191 percent for 1, 2, and 3 abortions, respectively, compared with no abortions after controlling for other reproductive outcomes and last pregnancy age."[25] This study demonstrates that having abortions actually increases the maternal death rate.

I have also heard the argument that people are not actually pro-life if they do not support low-income, single mothers and help them with the cost of raising a child they chose not to abort—that those people are just pro-birth, not pro-life. This is a philosophical view that I do not agree with. Let me explain why.

Pro-life, by definition, is opposition to abortion. I do believe that the church should continue to more fervently stand up and help single mothers, the poor, widows, etc. However, I do not believe that supporting low-income mothers is a pro-life topic—it is a quality-of-life topic. Being pro-life means standing against killing unborn children; standing for quality of life is helping those in need, such as low-income single mothers, the homeless, etc. Again, let me emphasize that churches and Christians are helping and should continue with more fervor to help support these women, but I believe this is a separate topic altogether.

Can an abortion clinic be pro-choice? I would say absolutely not. I am a primary care nurse practitioner, and I will state without a doubt that while every practice I have worked for may have had the patient's needs in mind, the bottom line (revenue) is also important; after all, a medical practice is a business.

In an abortion clinic setting, to keep the doors open and staff paid, a certain quota of abortions must be performed per month; it is a business, like any other healthcare clinic. Abby Johnson, a former Planned Parenthood clinic manager, describes this in detail in her book *Unplanned*.[26] In her book, she poses a question:

> Our goal at Planned Parenthood is to decrease the number of abortions by decreasing the number of unwanted pregnancies. That means family services—birth control. That is our stated goal. So why am I being asked, according to this budget, to increase my abortion revenue and thus my abortion client count?

She goes into detail about how she and other people who truly care about women's health and reducing abortions have been recruited to volunteer with Planned Parenthood because recruiters have told them that their focus was on preventing unwanted pregnancies, thus reducing abortions—not realizing that Planned Parenthood largely relies on abortions for its profits. And who can forget the recent video released in which Planned Parenthood's Senior Director of Medical Service, Dr. Deborah Nucatola, discussed the sale of fetal body parts while sipping her wine?[27] Money is made not just from the procedure, but also from the poor victims' body parts—very disturbing indeed.

With all of this said, ask yourself what your choice will be: life or abortion?

Chapter 6

WHEN THINGS GO WRONG

Dr. Steve Hammond (with Carrie Brown Campbell)

O ne of the reasons I went into obstetrics and gynecology was that delivering a baby was almost always a joyous occasion. So much of the practice of medicine deals with pain, sadness, and bad news, but for the most part obstetrics is a specialty of happiness. On the other hand, when the news is bad, I came to learn that sharing my patients' pain may be the most difficult of all situations in medicine. When the expectations of a joyous possibility are suddenly dashed, the grief seems to be compounded.

In our disposable society, there tends to be a knee-jerk response when a doctor says, "There is something wrong with your baby." The entire field of prenatal diagnosis (performing maternal blood and amniotic fluid testing to see if the baby has genetic defects) has come into being primarily to allow the opportunity for the parents to abort the baby if it is abnormal. The idea is that the baby can be destroyed so that the parents can try again for a "normal" baby—or at least not have to deal with the pain of a terminal outcome or the trouble and expense of raising a disabled child.

One of the most common defects is Down syndrome (also called trisomy 21). It is caused when there is an extra 21st chromosome, and this results in a child with both physical and mental handicaps. Though most parents of Down syndrome infants will tell you of the blessings that such a child brings to their family, many parents feel that they can't cope with the challenges that such a child presents. Many choose to abort the child instead of considering delivery or adoption, and while many couples would gladly adopt a child with Down syndrome, some parents choose abortion instead of adoption.

How should a Christian respond to such a situation? Certainly not with judgment or condemnation. No one can say how they might respond if placed in that situation and encouraged to abort by their family or healthcare provider. They might think that abortion is the best choice and never consider other options. I think that we, as Christians, should start with the premise that all human life is sacred and created in the image of God. While the culture at large might disagree with this premise, this must be our starting point. When counseling others, we should always respect their point of view and never seek to impose our will on them, but lovingly seek to help bear their burden. This should never change what we believe to be true, and it should influence our advice if it is requested.

I have a dear friend who endured a heart-wrenching ordeal a few years ago. When she agreed to share her story, I was elated . . . not only because it shows how a true believer who has an abiding trust in Jesus Christ should respond to such a tragedy, but also because it can help people understand, as in the story of Job, how God loves it when we trust Him despite our circumstances. May her story encourage you to believe that there is a silver lining to every dark cloud for a believer. If you ever encounter someone who is struggling with this kind of decision, remember the story of Anna Suzanne, Carrie Brown's first daughter, which she shares below:

I was 17 weeks pregnant with my first child when we discovered that our baby had a lethal condition. I remember the morning perfectly. Our appointment was at 10:00 a.m. I was wearing black leggings, a flowing tan top, and leather boots. I had been so sick that morning, but I felt like the cutest pregnant girl around. I just knew that I needed to be well dressed for this doctor's appointment because this was the day we had been so excited for—were we going to be bringing home a baby boy or a baby girl? I know it's silly, but I was so excited to find out. My husband, Nick, and I went into the ultrasound room, and the sweet ultrasound technician started the process.

She was quiet, but this was my first pregnancy, so I didn't know what was routine versus what was abnormal, and I assumed that all was normal. After several minutes of silence, I asked if she could tell us the baby's gender. She said, "I believe it's a girl. Let me go get the doctor." Again, I was new to this, so I didn't realize that the doctor doesn't regularly come into the ultrasound room initially. We were thrilled, and I was already picturing a sweet little curly-haired girl with a big white bow in her hair. Then our doctor came in, and that's when my entire world stopped.

My obstetrician is not only my physician, but she is also one of my closest friends. I will never forget her face when she walked in the room. There were tears in her eyes, and she looked heartbroken. She walked over, kneeled in front of me, and grabbed my hands. All I remember her saying was, "I'm so sorry." There may have been more (I'm sure there was), but she didn't have to say much. I remember screaming and running out of the room. The only thing I can remember saying was, "I can't do this!". . . over and over again.

Nick called my parents to tell them what was going on, and they came to get us from the clinic to drive us to the hospital, where we would see the high-risk perinatal physician. My parents are wonderful. They're the kind of parents that everyone would love to have. They are open, honest, kind, and amazing—I may be biased, but they truly are the best. Because of them, I was not unfamiliar with the grief that comes with the loss of a baby. I was raised with a wonderful sister, Sarah, who is 10 years my elder, but my parents have another daughter who was born five years before me. Anna Kathryn had trisomy 13 and lived for only 17 hours. I had always admired both of my parents' strength, but I certainly did not want to test my own.

The high-risk perinatal doctor's office is on the same floor as the maternity unit and until recently, it shared a waiting room with labor and delivery. This meant that when we were sent to the waiting room to wait on the doctor who was going to give us specific information about the condition that would most likely take our daughter from us, we were waiting with all of the families and friends of those in labor with healthy babies. I vividly remember seeing a bouquet of pink balloons in that waiting room. It was awful. Thankfully, my mother went directly back across the hall, mustered up every bit of "mama bear" in her, and demanded that we be allowed to wait somewhere else. Soon, a nurse came into the room. She could see the anguish in us all, and she grabbed my face and said, "You will survive this. You don't feel like you will, I know. But you will."

She proceeded to tell us about her son, who had passed away a few years before. He had trisomy 21 and passed away before birth. There I was, in this tiny room with two other women— my mother included—who had survived the death of a baby. It was the first moment that I realized I could do this. I had to do this. I had no choice.

I was soon sent into an ultrasound room, where another sweet ultrasound technician began a very thorough ultrasound on my baby girl. She measured every bone, watched blood flow through her heart, and took all kinds of measurements. It was simultaneously amazing, terrible, and beautiful to watch this sweet baby move around inside of me, knowing that there was something horribly wrong.

After my ultrasound, we met with Dr. Wagner, who is one of the kindest men I have ever known. He gave us our child's official diagnosis—a lethal form of skeletal dysplasia. To put it in extreme layman's terms, her bones were too small, including the bones in her rib cage, which meant that her lungs would not have room to expand outside of the womb. Because of this, she would not be able to live in this world, or at least not for long, but it also meant that she would be able to survive inside of the womb, and that I would quite possibly carry her to full term. There was potential for her to live a few days, possibly months, but most likely, she would pass away before birth or after a few hours. There were a lot of unknowns— too many unknowns. I am a planner, and there was no way to plan for this.

At this point, I was 17 weeks pregnant, and I believe the gestational limit for abortion was 20 or 21 weeks. Dr. Wagner informed us that he legally had to give us the option to terminate the pregnancy. He told us that we only had a few weeks to decide, and I remember him also saying that while he had to legally give us that option, he also had seen many women choose both ways, and the women who chose to terminate often had long-term repercussions like divorce and depression while most women who chose to continue with their pregnancies did not. Would termination have been an easier

decision in that moment? It's quite possible.
But I knew that I needed to carry her and love
her as long as I could. I had just watched my
daughter, however physically flawed, move
around inside of my belly. I had seen her move
her tiny little arms and legs. I loved her, and she
was mine. So there we were. Decision made. I
would continue with the pregnancy for as long
as God would allow with a child that I may
never know outside of my womb. I have never
been more certain of a decision.

The next 17 weeks were the most grueling
weeks of my life. I am barely five feet tall, so a
pregnant belly really stands out on me. I also
developed polyhydramios, which means that
I had a lot of extra fluid in the amniotic sac,
resulting in a huge belly. People always say
that you're not supposed to ask if someone
is pregnant unless you are really sure—well,
people were really sure about me, and they
asked. Everyone I saw asked how far along I
was, if it was a boy or girl, and what her name
was. They gave me advice on diapers, formula,
breastfeeding, and all of the other normal things
that people tell pregnant women. All of these
people had the best of intentions and could not
have known that I didn't need that advice. They
didn't know that I wasn't excited, that I was

terrified, or that I was completely heartbroken that I would not be needing diapers, a car seat, or a crib. I went to the doctor weekly, and each time was as difficult as the last. It was truly a devastating 17 weeks, and I did not know if I would ever be joyful again.

On March 8, 2013, I woke up around 8:00 a.m. with contractions. They were far apart, but I knew that I was in labor and that this was the day that I had dreaded for so long. We called Lolly, my obstetrician friend who would deliver our baby, and she told us to go to the hospital. We checked in, and they confirmed that I was in labor. The doctors and nurses could not have been more accommodating or empathetic. They understood the magnitude of this situation and treated us with such kindness. The majority of the day was a blur. We were visited by so many precious friends and family, and we were prayed over by so many people.

Around midnight, Lolly came in and broke my water. I remember feeling her moving, and then I remember it slowing down. I asked her if Nick and I could have a minute before I started pushing. I can still remember being in that hospital bed with my precious husband's arms around me, feeling our baby move.

Shortly thereafter, the doctor came back in and said it was time to push. She was breach, so her feet came out first. I remember looking at Lolly as soon as part of her was out, and I can still picture her face. She looked directly at me with watery eyes and shook her head slowly. I knew she was gone. It was the most peaceful moment of my entire life. I cannot possibly explain it, and the memory will forever bring chills and tears to my eyes.

At 1:24 a.m. on March 9, 2013, Anna Suzanne Campbell came into this world and directly into the loving arms of Jesus. For the few hours that we were able to keep her with us, I just couldn't believe the depth of my pain in contrast to the fullness of the peace I experienced. My last moment of seeing my daughter was as the nurse came to take her away. She picked her up so tenderly and carried her out of our dark room into the light of the hospital hallway. It was completely beautiful and a moment I will never forget.

Looking back, even after just a few years, it is amazing to see how present God was in the depths of my heartbreak and how He used my pain to draw me to Him. I felt the power of prayer so strongly. I was weak through my pregnancy, but the prayers of my family and friends kept me going when I didn't think I could.

During my pregnancy, I studied Hannah and felt such a connection with her because of her humanity. She wouldn't eat and cried when Penninah taunted her. I love the language used when describing her prayers to the Lord as she begged for a child. "In her deep anguish, she prayed" . . . "she wept bitterly to the Lord." Even in her vow to God, she asked Him to look upon her misery and grant her a child. When I was crying out to God, I was miserable, and I appreciated that she had been, too. Hannah was considered obedient, and God heard her cries. It gave me so much freedom to be really honest with God. It was in those honest, ugly, tearful conversations with God that my relationship with Him grew. It brought me to a place of trust. I really trusted His promise for me in Jeremiah 29:11. "For I know the plans I have for you . . . plans to prosper you and not to harm you, plans to give you hope and a future." It was so freeing.

It's amazing that even when we think we have shut down, God can still speak to us and guide us. I was angry with Him—very angry. I could not understand why my baby had to die. I thought I could be a good mother, and my husband would be a good father. I remember thinking, "Why me?" I wondered what I had done that I deserved such punishment. It wasn't until after Anna Suzanne's birth that I realized that God had not punished me. . . . He had **chosen** me.

Ten months after Anna Suzanne's death, on our fourth wedding anniversary, I discovered that I was once again pregnant. I was both overjoyed and completely anxious. I waited a week before going into the clinic for my first prenatal appointment. As I lay on the table, waiting for them to conduct my ultrasound, I could not contain my nervousness. What if this baby died, too? Would I be able to survive again? I was quickly reminded of Jeremiah 29:11, and my nerves calmed to at least a tolerable level. Soon after the warm gel hit my belly, the ultrasound technician smiled, tilted her head a bit, and said, "Well, I see two sacs. I think you have two babies in there." TWINS! We were told not to get our hopes up as I was still very early in my pregnancy, and often both twins don't survive, but I had prayed for twins since Nick and I had started discussing trying to get pregnant again. I knew that pregnancy would be so anxiety-ridden for me, and in my completely non-medically educated thoughts, twins sounded ideal! I had told Lolly to pray for twins for me from the time I started praying for them. She responded with a quick, "No, I am praying for one normal, easy pregnancy." And there I was, 10 months after such a devastating loss, pregnant with twins. I just couldn't believe that God had answered such a specific prayer.

Pregnancy after loss is hard. It is nerve-racking and just plain scary. I was a high-risk patient because of Anna Suzanne's condition, so I frequently went to see the high-risk doctor in addition to attending my regular appointments. We were told that at our 12-week ultrasound, they would be able to measure long bones, and from those measurements, they would be able to rule out skeletal dysplasia. When week 12 arrived, I watched the screen as the ultrasound began, and there they were: two perfectly formed babies with perfectly normal bones. I cannot describe the relief, and I could not hold back the tears.

As our 20-week appointment approached, we had calmed a bit, knowing that our twins did not have skeletal dysplasia, and were now able to enjoy some of the excitement that is supposed to come alongside pregnancy. This was the fetal assessment ultrasound, and it would be the day when we would know if we were having boys, girls, or one of each. My mother just knew it was one of each, and I was convinced it was two boys. I am not one to place too much importance on the sex of the baby, but even so, it is fun to know. As much as I hated that I felt this way and didn't want to admit it, I told Nick the night before we went to the appointment that I secretly hoped that at least one of our babies was a girl. Even though it was brief, I had imagined my life as a mother of a sweet little ponytailed girl with bows, and I had imagined Nick as a dad wrapped around his daughter's finger.

As it turns out, our daughters at age 2 just barely have enough hair for a ponytail, their bows look great, and their daddy is completely wrapped around their fingers. Every time I look at our precious girls, I cannot believe how much God loves me. He took my heartbreak and my anguish and turned it into something beautiful. I know that I am a better mother to my twins because I was first a mother to their big sister.

Anna Suzanne Campbell is my daughter, regardless of whether she ever took a breath outside of the womb, and I am so thankful that God made me her mother.

Chapter 7

THE TRUTH ABOUT THE LIES WOMEN ARE TOLD

Emily LaBonte

1. UNFORTUNATE TRUTH: I'll get kicked out of school.

I grew up in a small town—an unfortunately pretentious environment. Many people acted as if they had everything together instead of being honest about their struggles (as they say in the South, you don't air your dirty laundry in public). This is largely due to the Bible Belt culture, where everyone struggles silently while pretending that everything in their life is great. It is also due to the way that people handle certain situations, and teenage pregnancy is a good example of this.

I now live in Las Vegas, Nevada, and sin is openly accepted here more than anywhere else I have lived or traveled. People are open and honest about their sin; there is no reason to hide it in the infamous "Sin City," which I am praying will become "Saved City." This is so different from living in the South, where I grew up. While people in the South often try to hide their shortcomings, people in Las Vegas are very transparent, and this is honestly refreshing at times. One nuance about growing up in the Bible Belt and getting a Christian education is that we were taught as youth that hidden sin is better than transparent sin. Let me explain.

People who sinned and were able to keep it secret did not get in trouble, but if you were accidentally caught or if you intentionally admitted your faults, you were chastised. This was the case with the administration in the private school I attended in particular. For example, girls who got pregnant and decided to keep their babies were kicked out of school, but girls who hid their pregnancies and had abortions were able to continue school. What a shame!

This was a high school that was founded and supposedly functioning on Christian principles, yet young girls, influenced by school policy, were willing to kill their unborn children for the sake of perfect attendance and saving face at school—all while the girls who came forward with their unintended pregnancies were expelled. Do not get me wrong; there should be reprimands when students do something that is against school policy; however, when it comes to life, a student should be supported in the utmost way to complete her education if she decides to move forward with a pregnancy—not be encouraged to abort her child.

2. LIE: I'll escape all consequences of this pregnancy if I just get rid of it.

More and more evidence is surfacing that demonstrates that women who have had abortions suffer higher rates of psychiatric illness, breast cancer, maternal death, future pre-term birth, and autoimmune diseases. In fact, 139 studies spanning 40 years demonstrate a statistically significant increased risk for preterm birth associated with elective abortion. Women with histories of abortion experience an 81-percent increased risk of mental health problems, including depression, anxiety, suicide, and substance abuse. Interruption of a pregnancy by abortion arrests the cycle that occurs in breast tissue during a normal pregnancy, increasing the risk of breast cancer. The later in pregnancy that an abortion occurs, the higher the risk becomes. The more abortions that are performed on the same woman, the higher the risk. Many studies have also shown an association with increased maternal death rates due to abortion —just the opposite of what was claimed to happen if abortion were to have been legalized (as indeed it was) in the 1970s.[28]

Another way to look at this is scripturally. Hebrews 12:6 says, "For the Lord disciplines the one he loves, and chastises every son whom he receives." And Paul in Galatians 6:7 says, "Do not be deceived: God is not mocked, for whatever one sows, that will he also reap." This does not change the fact that Jesus died on the cross so that our Father in heaven could forgive us; through Jesus we are saved. Praise His name!

However, God still disciplines His people when they disobey. This was very evident in the Old Testament when His chosen people wandered around in the wilderness for 40 years, but it is still very applicable today. He is a loving Father and shows us His love through discipline when we need it. I, too, have received discipline from the Lord, and it was not pleasant, but it was ultimately for my good and His glory. However, I did not escape the consequences of my sin.

3. LIE: I should not have to carry a baby to term if I am raped.

Let me start by re-emphasizing that rape victims rarely become pregnant as a result. It is incredibly difficult for a woman to become pregnant under normal circumstances, but the stress and trauma involved in rape make it considerably more difficult. As discussed in a previous chapter, a study found that fewer than one percent of women seeking abortions did so due to rape. However, all women are significant. Even one pregnancy resulting from rape is important. As a woman, I cannot imagine the turmoil that would result from this situation, but I do believe that having an abortion would only make it worse.

The truth is that many women regret abortions and suffer mental repercussions because of them—often leading to anxiety, depression, substance abuse, and even suicide.

Consider this scenario: a woman has an abortion because she cannot bear to see the face of her rapist in her child's face, but then she begins to consider that the rape was not her child's fault and begins to regret her decision, sending her into depression. Now she is not only dealing with the trauma of rape but is also dealing with depression, having realized that she has aborted an innocent child.

Now consider a raped woman birthing and keeping her child. The mother begins to bond with her baby, which is natural, and, in turn, this helps her heal from the trauma of rape. Consider the following Scripture: "Yet she will be saved through childbearing—if they continue in faith and love and holiness, with self-control" (1 Timothy 2:15). This Scripture is not talking about salvation; it is talking about becoming more like Christ through sanctification.

I am a mother, and by becoming a mother I have indeed become a more devout follower of Christ. I have learned mountains more about selflessness and the love of God by becoming a mother. However, for those who do not feel called to motherhood, adoption is always another option.

4. LIE: I can't raise or afford a child (or another child) by myself.

It's difficult to raise a child as a single parent, but it can be so rewarding. Pregnancy support centers are available to help, and if someone falls within the poverty line, government assistance can provide financial help. Getting involved in a local church is also a great way to gain support from people who care, and many brothers and sisters in Christ would be willing to lend a helping hand. The point is that no one has to raise a child alone. You can find the support you need by engaging in your community. I have personally known many women in my church community who kept their children in spite of living in poverty, never regretting their choice. Many of these women gained support from both the church and the government. Christ also promises us that we will never be alone. In Joshua 1:9, God speaks to Joshua, saying, "Have I not commanded you? Be strong and courageous. Do not be frightened, and do not be dismayed, for the LORD your God is with you wherever you go." Rest assured, our God sees us in our circumstances and is with us wherever we go.

5. LIE: Wouldn't it be better for my child not to be born into poverty?

I think the main question here is this: Does money determine quality of life? My resounding answer is no. I know rich people who are miserable and poor people who are joyful. One's attitude and finding her purpose determine quality of life, not her socioeconomic status. Believing that it would be better to abort a child instead of raising that same child in poverty is similar to believing that it would be better to have a mass killing of all poor and homeless people instead of allowing them to live and have a chance to succeed. I'll turn your attention to Matthew 6:31–33, where Jesus Himself is speaking:

> Therefore do not be anxious, saying, "What shall we eat?" or "What shall we drink?" or "What shall we wear?" For the Gentiles seek after all these things, and your heavenly Father knows that you need them all. But seek first the kingdom of God and his righteousness, and all these things will be added to you.

Believers, let's have more faith that the God of the universe will provide for our needs; let's not worry about monetary things; let's seek His kingdom with all our hearts!

6. LIE: I found out that my child will be born with a disability. It will be better to abort that child and try again.

Consider the following statements[29] from Charlotte Fien, a young woman with Down syndrome who made a plea to the United Nations:

I am not suffering.

I am not ill. None of my friends who have Down's syndrome are suffering, either. We live happy lives.

We just have an extra chromosome.

We are still human beings. We are not monsters. Don't be afraid of us. . . . Please don't try to kill us all off.

I have personally worked with people with many different challenges who are some of the most carefree, joyous people I've ever met. They are happy to live with their "disabilities." Many times, it is the parent who does not want to raise a child with a disability. May we give up our selfish attitudes toward parenthood and raise the children whom God himself designs for us. Let's not abort children based on their lack of abilities or their differences.

In Carrie Brown's story in the chapter "When Things Go Wrong," a mother chooses to carry her terminal unborn baby to term, knowing the outcome and realizing from the beginning that her baby will not live long past birth or even make it through birth. She experienced healing beyond human comprehension because of her selfless act and her trust in the Lord. She got to hold her baby in her arms for a few hours and experience healing from the Lord. It's amazing what happens when we decide to give our wills and plans to God.

It is also important to note that undesirability is not a moral basis for abortion. Undesirability can come in many forms: a child with a disability, the gender that you did not hope for, the number of babies you did not plan on, the timing not being convenient, etc. Also, "unplanned" does not equate to "unwanted"—this supposed correlation is a misnomer. An unplanned baby for one couple may be another couple's wanted baby. God calls us all desirable. He sent His Son to die for all of us (the whole world) before we even knew Him. He chose us before creation to live holy lives for Him. In Ephesians 1:4 Paul says ". . . even as he chose us in him before the foundation of the world, that we should be holy and blameless before him." He chose us because He desires a relationship with us! What a loving God! He loves all of us, even those we might call undesirable. Let us seek to love one another through the lens of our Father.

7. LIE: Abortion prevents child abuse.

Those claiming that abortion is needed to reduce child abuse must contend with the empirical reality that child abuse increased by more than 500 percent in the decade following *Roe v. Wade*. In fact, in less than a decade after Roe, child abuse had already risen by more than 500 percent. These stats come right from the U.S. Department of Health and Human Services.[30]

Simply put, abortion does not prevent child abuse. Child abuse rates have risen since abortion was legalized in the 1970s.

8. LIE: If I continue a pregnancy out of wedlock, no man will ever want me.

The first problem with this statement is that it is centered around identity. If you are pregnant out of wedlock, your identity is not found in your sin—it is found in your Savior! While the world may think less of you, what really matters is what the Lord thinks of you, and He calls you loved—a royal priestess, chosen, a new creation. In 2 Corinthians 5:17 Paul says, "Therefore, if anyone is in Christ, he is a new creation. The old has passed away; behold, the new has come." He believes it, and we should, too. Also believe that God does not want anyone to abort a baby. If you are pregnant, He loves your baby as much as He loves you. He has a purpose for your life and for your baby's life. Try to forget what the world will say; it only matters what Christ says.

The second problem in this statement is that it is centered around plans for your future. If God wants a woman to have a man in her life, then she will have one. As expressed in Jeremiah 29:11, "For I know the plans I have for you, declares the LORD, plans for welfare and not for evil, to give you a future and a hope." We cannot thwart God's plan for us—whether with a man or without one. And we are wanted by the King of kings!

9. LIE: All of the women in my family have had abortions, so it's okay for me to have one, too.

As we read in Romans 2:6, "[God] will render to each one according to his works." This means that we will not be given leniency just because we thought a decision was okay; instead, the Lord will judge each person based on her actions. We do not get a pass. We are each accountable for our own actions. Just because the people you look up to think an abortion is okay does not make it right. Seek what God says about it in His Word first! I am convinced that you will find He does not approve. Also, consider this: our actions can be influenced by prior generations, and our actions can affect generations to come. God speaks to Moses in Exodus 34:6–7, stating:

> . . . the LORD, the LORD, a God merciful and gracious, slow to anger, and abounding in steadfast love and faithfulness, keeping steadfast love for thousands, forgiving iniquity and transgression and sin, but who will by no means clear the guilty, visiting the iniquity of the fathers on the children and the children's children, to the third and the fourth generation.

God will not let the guilty go unpunished. Our actions today can affect generations to come in a bad or good way. In the case of abortion, generations can be annihilated even before birth. In the chapter titled "Dany's Story," we will see how the actions of one woman's grandmother affected the actions of her mom, which in turn affected Dany in a powerful, life-altering way. Our actions today can impact our children's children's children. If your family has a history of abortion, I urge you to change the course. Make a stand to stop abortion in your generation, and change the future for generations to come!

10. LIE: It's my body; I can do what I want with it.

Those who are believers forfeit rights to their bodies when they submit to Christ as Lord at the time of their salvation. Our bodies are sanctuaries for the Holy Spirit to inhabit and direct as He will. We should honor the Lord with our bodies and the actions of our bodies. Also, it is not just a woman's body to be considered; it is the body of the unborn child that is the primary focus. We are discussing abortion, not suicide; if a woman's body were the primary focus, we would be discussing another topic altogether. Please refer to the chapter titled "Sanctity of Life" for further explanation on this topic.

11. LIE: My parents say I have to get an abortion, so I have to obey them.

The Bible is very clear about honoring our parents. The Bible mentions in many places the importance of honoring our father and mother; this is so important that it is one of the Ten Commandments. We must always honor and obey them . . . as long as this does not contradict the way we are instructed to live by the Word of God. Ultimately, we have to honor God as our heavenly Father. If our parents would have us do something that would not please God, we must obey God first. We can respect our parents, even when we disagree with them. In the instance of abortion, if your parents want you to get an abortion, know that God does not, so you must first obey God. Thankfully, the law does protect minors in this. No one can force another person to have an abortion—that is the law, and it does apply to minors.

12. UNFORTUNATE TRUTH: I can undergo an abortion procedure without telling my parents.

This is sad to me. In many states, no parental consent or notification is required at all for a minor to obtain an abortion. I cannot imagine being a young teenager in the scary situation of an unwanted pregnancy and not telling my parents. I do not think that I, as a young teen, would even have been mature enough to make the complicated decision of carrying a pregnancy to term (keeping the baby or putting the baby up for adoption) versus having an abortion. However, this is legal. As fear sinks into the mind of a pregnant young teenager, that fear can become blinding. They may think their only option is abortion when, in fact, their parents would be supportive of either keeping the baby or offering the baby for adoption.

It is also my opinion, as a parent of a daughter, that if she were in this situation it would be my right to know, especially if she is still a minor. After all, I have to consent to anything else she would have done medically—even the administration of Tylenol in a medical clinic—and I am obligated to provide for her in every way as a parent—financially, emotionally, mentally, physically, and spiritually. I am even obligated to consent to medical care for her because children and adolescents are not considered to be developed enough to make complex decisions regarding their health.

However, abortion is the exception to that rule in some states. As a parent, I want to know if my child is considering abortion, as it is against my core values, and I would do everything in my power to stop her. I feel that I have the right to try to convince my child to choose a better way. This is a life-and-death matter; children and adolescents should not be given the right to choose abortion without parental counsel, but this is an unfortunate reality today.

13. LIE: I must have an abortion to break the "teen mom, no dad" cycle for my children.

As a young woman who grew up with a teen mother and without a father figure, my dear friend Kelcey particularly relates to this lie, as it is a lie she believed (see the chapter titled "Kelcey's Story"). She thought that abortion was her only option; she had not even considered adoption. Adoption in this situation is the best way to break the "teen mom, no dad" cycle, especially if you are placing your child into the home of a couple who wants a child but cannot have one themselves.

Another way to break the cycle is by keeping your child and praying fervently that your child will be the one to break that cycle instead of ending it altogether with abortion. Instilling truth from the Word of God into your child (biblical marriage is the best setting to raise children) and praying for your child are powerful ways to break negative cycles in families. And there is power in praying and speaking truth! James 5:16 counsels us, "Therefore, confess your sins to one another and pray for one another, that you may be healed. The prayer of a righteous person has great power as it is working."

14. LIE: I do not have the support system to raise a child on my own.

This is simply a lie. Financial issues were addressed earlier in this chapter (see No. 4, above), but there are also shelters for women and their children across the country that offer assistance for housing. Most importantly, as believers we have the support of the local church. Many church families would be willing to help a single mom in any way they could. Couples in the church would offer to babysit if you needed a break, give you a baby shower for things you need, and offer more advice on how to raise your child than you would probably want to hear. This is our obligation as the body of Christ—to love and build each other up and help those who are in need.

15. LIE: If my life is at risk, it is okay for me to have a late-term abortion.

There seems to be a lot of confusion between late-term abortion and early induction. Any child can be induced early in the third trimester, as they are at the point of viability (and, if healthy, will most likely survive). If the mother's life is at risk, most reasonable obstetricians would induce early, as the primary intention is to save the mother, not kill the child. There is no medical reason to give a lethal injection intra-abdominally into the baby's heart, killing the baby prior to birth. Regardless, if the mother has a late-term abortion or is induced early, she still has to labor and deliver the baby. Why would anyone who has to go through the pain of labor want to kill the child first? And if, for some reason, a mistake is made and the baby is born alive, the mother has the right to have the baby resuscitated or put on "comfort care" until the baby dies.

There is another form of late-term abortion that is still used in some states; it is called partial-birth abortion. In this scenario, the mother labors, delivers the baby breech (feet first) except for the head, and then the baby's brain is sucked out, the skull is crushed, and the body is fully removed from the birth canal. This is an absolutely brutal practice.

There is a very distinct difference between early induction to save a woman's life and late-term abortion. Third-trimester C-section or early induction is always the way to go in the very rare situation that the mother's life is at risk. Inducing labor early is already legal in any of the 50 states when the mother's life is in jeopardy. There is no reason to have a law allowing late-term abortion because there are other medical alternatives.[31]

Chapter 8

WHOSE RIGHTS?

Dr. Steve Hammond

T here is so much said about a woman's right to choose that the situation invites some thought as to how this "right" became the point of the spear in the abortion argument. It goes something like this: "Abortion is a medical procedure, and the choice to have or not to have the baby should be left up to the woman and her physician."

While abortion is a medical procedure, it is much more than that. First, it arguably involves two lives. Those who dispute that an unborn baby is not a life must explain why, in some states, if a person kills a woman who is pregnant, they can be prosecuted for both lives. Does the fact that the baby inside the murdered woman was wanted by the woman's family change the baby's status from non-person to person solely on that basis? Only a convolution of the law to accommodate the political correctness of abortion can explain this dichotomy.

Clearly, not all medical procedures are moral or legal. Consider practices like infanticide, selling

115

narcotics for profit, or harvesting body parts for sale. To state that we should turn our backs on these things because a medical professional does them or says they are permissible is foolishness. The law has something to say about medical practice, as it should. While it is true that the Supreme Court decreed that the denial of abortion infringed on the pregnant woman's freedom of privacy, it made no claims about the morality of the procedure.

We have all heard the phrase "You can't legislate morality." While this is true in the sense that you can't pass a law that will cause people to act morally, it is clear that many laws are based on morality. Societies pass laws forbidding murder, prostitution, and driving while intoxicated because these acts are immoral; they injure and otherwise risk the health, life, or well-being of another person; and they do not promote the general welfare of the population.

True human rights, such as those delineated in the Declaration of Independence and the Constitution of the United States, are given by God. This is actually stated in the Declaration of Independence, written by Thomas Jefferson: "We hold these truths to be self-evident, that all men are created equal, that they are endowed by their Creator with certain unalienable rights, that among these are life, liberty and the pursuit of happiness."[32]

Why did Jefferson say that the rights came from God and not from the government? We can only speculate that he considered that rights given by God superseded those that a government might allow. Perhaps he considered that while government might give and later rescind certain rights, the rights given by God cannot be taken away. Perhaps he could see a day in the future when those in power in the government that he and the other founders were establishing might create a law that would infringe on the rights of some of its citizens. Therefore, at least in the context of the opening lines of the Declaration of Independence, Jefferson held that our nation's founders were addressing incontrovertible rights and not rights imposed by a legislature or court.

We must ask the question: Can so-called rights imposed by the government fail to reflect the rights given by God or even directly oppose them? There are many examples of laws that have been rescinded, but perhaps the most infamous is the 1857 7–2 ruling by the Supreme Court in the Dred Scott case. In effect, *Dred Scott v. Sanford* ruled for only the second time in history that a duly passed law of the US Congress was unconstitutional and decreed that the descendants of slaves brought to the United States could not become citizens of the United States and had no right to sue in federal court.

This decision remained until 1866, when it was overturned by the 14th Amendment, which gave full rights to all African Americans. The point of this example is that if we look at the rights granted by government, we must understand that when they are at odds with God's law, ultimately God's law must prevail. Also we should realize that rights given by God are always in concert with His character. Therefore, if we claim that we have rights that are derived from government but are at odds with God's character, they will sooner or later come to be overturned.

As Christians, we understand that this will either be when government returns to God, or ultimately in the final judgment by God himself. Government will return to God when the hearts of the people first turn to Him. Hearts that belong to God will want and elect a government that reveres Him.

Chapter 9

DANY'S STORY

Emily LaBonte (with Dany)

I first met Dany (or Trivia, as everyone calls her) in mid-2017 at one of the many primary care clinics in my work rotation in Las Vegas. Dany is an atmosphere-changer—the kind of person who changes the mood or tone of the room just by being present. Joy, kindness, and the love of the Lord pour out of her, and people are automatically in a better mood just by being around her. She is a powerful, Holy Spirit-filled believer who has become a dear friend to me.

When I first started writing this book, I spoke with Dany about it, and she shared her story with me, which I am honored to be able to include in this book. Her story specifically addresses the coercion factor that influences many women and young girls to have abortions, in addition to the remorse they feel following the procedure. Dany's story is so powerful, and I pray that you will open your heart and mind as you read it, below:

I grew up in an area of Chicago where group housing was very prevalent. My family was always the first to church on Sunday morning. We went to a Missionary Baptist church, but unfortunately, the pastors at my church would not speak up against many controversial topics, including abortion. They remained silent on the topic but preached that God wants abundant life for His children and wants His children to be happy. They would also say that they could not judge us, so they would tell us to do what was needed for the benefit of the family, including the situation of an unwanted pregnancy.

My family often had visiting relatives who would come and go, and unfortunately, there were instances of molestation. We also experienced quite a bit of teenage pregnancy. A lot of girls in my neighborhood, school, and church thought it was OK to sleep with their boyfriends because their relatives were molesting and raping them. In my family and culture, a young woman who got pregnant outside of marriage was considered damaged—a whore, a "loose" girl, and unwanted, among many other things. I was told by my family that no man would want me if I ever got pregnant because real men want to start a family and not inherit a ready-made family. I was also told that I would not be able to better myself if I got pregnant . . . I would be on government assistance for the rest of my life, and I would be worth nothing without a job. My family told me these things as a scare tactic to make me fearful of dating, sex, and pregnancy. This was a common belief in my community as well. The fear of these social stigmas impact[s] many people so strongly that they end up doing more harm than good in an attempt to avoid falling into them. As a result, a lot of girls that I knew had abortions because they didn't want a bad name. And because many of their mothers, grandmothers, and great grandmothers had abortions— mine included—they felt justified in having abortions, too.

I was 16 years old and living with my grandmother in 1990, and I got pregnant by the first person I ever slept with. I didn't even know I was pregnant, and when my grandmother noticed, she said, "I see that baby heartbeat in your throat." She made me go to the pharmacy and buy a pregnancy test. It was positive, and she told me to leave because she needed to collect herself. At that point, I went to live with my mother.

When I told my boyfriend about the baby, he wanted to keep our baby as much as I did.

We were so excited and had plans of raising our baby together. He wanted to be the kind of father to his child that he did not have growing up.

One day, my mother told me that she was taking me to the clinic to check on the baby. When I got there, I was strapped down to a table, my legs were placed in stirrups, and I was forced to get an abortion. The staff told me that "the woman who paid" did not pay for anesthesia, so I had no pain medication during or after the procedure. I felt everything, and it hurt badly. I would try to buck and squirm, and they held me down harder. The doctor used his shoulder to keep my legs up and open, and the nurse lay on top of me and told me that I was only hurting myself more by not being still. Afterward, they left me by myself to calm down.

The next day, my mother locked the gate to the front door of our house so I couldn't get out to tell my grandmother what had happened. I started bleeding so badly that I drenched my clothes and my bed with blood. My stepdad didn't know what had happened, and he checked on me two or three days later because I was not getting out of bed. When he saw that all I could do was lie in bed, he called my mom, and she met us at the hospital. They packed me with female packing and sent me home, and I had the packing removed the next day. When my boyfriend found out what happened, he was heartbroken, and he broke up with me. He was so upset that he called me every ungodly thing in the book, told me to get out of his face, threatened me, and even threatened my mother. He was so hurt. Honestly, I think we would still be together today had I not been forced to have that abortion.

As a Christian, I want to be able to say that I have been totally healed. I have really struggled with forgiving my mother, and our relationship has gone through some trials due to everything that happened. I have blamed her for a long time because if she hadn't done what she did to me at 16 years old, things would be so different. My body was traumatized by the abortion. After [my] having a major abdominal surgery years later, the surgeon told me that there were so many adhesions and so much scar tissue in and around my reproductive organs that it looked like I had a "back alley" abortion in my past. I believe that the trauma from the abortion and all of the residual scar tissue are the reasons why I am now infertile. To try to get pregnant, I've gone as far as trying three rounds of in vitro fertilization, but the eggs wouldn't attach to my uterus because of all of the scar tissue.

At my annual woman's health exam, it feels like a fire of emotions building inside of me. Memories of the abortion still flood my mind. I'm now 42 years old, and I'm still not over it. I regret everything. If my baby were still alive, I would have a 24-year-old child. This makes it very difficult for me to be around pregnant girls at work. I can't even bring myself to go see my coworker's sweet baby that was recently born; it just hurts too much.

After the surgeon told me about all of my scar tissue, I lashed out at my mom, told her I can't have babies because of her, and asked her why she did that to me. She told me that my grandmother was influenced by her sisters to force my mother to have an abortion, too. In my family and many others, this is a generational problem. My mom did it to me because it had been done to her, and she thought it was OK. My mom got pregnant with me less than six months after she was forced to have an abortion by my grandmother, and I'm the oldest of six children.

I think my mom's way of asking for forgiveness is asking me if I want to adopt, but I'm just not ready. I love my mother with every bone in my body, and after all of this time, I have finally forgiven her! Praise God—only He has been able to make that possible. While I may not be totally healed yet, I trust with all of my being that the Lord will totally heal me one day.

One thing I have learned is that abortion should not be a shortcut to eliminate a problem. If women get pregnant outside of marriage, they should be encouraged to trust the Lord with their future and their child's future. We should trust that the Lord will provide in all situations. My mother told me that if I had my baby, I wouldn't have gone as far in life as I have. But I know myself, and I would have shown her and the rest of my family that I could have made it. I would have finished school; I know I would have. I would have been able to show my family that everything they thought was going to go wrong could actually go right. I just wish that I had been given the chance to try. The saddest part is that this sort of thing happens to a lot of girls. Do you know how many Danys are out there? Thousands . . . there are thousands of girls with my story.

What a thought: there are thousands of girls who are forced to have abortions and deeply regret it decades later. As Dr. and Mrs. J. C. Willke have said, "It is easier to scrape the baby out of the mother's womb than to scrape the memory of the baby out of her mind."[33]

As we can see in Dany's story, not all abortions are outcomes of a woman's decision for herself and her unborn child. Mothers force daughters to have abortions, pimps force prostitutes to have abortions, and boyfriends and husbands force their partners to have abortions. There are literally thousands of stories like this among women who have found themselves in similar situations.

While it is not legal for anyone to be forced to have an abortion, it still frequently occurs. No medical practice is perfect. Not all patients are informed of the risks of abortions, and not all medical facilities screen to ensure a patient is not being coerced or forced to have an abortion. As you can see in Dany's case, she did not want the procedure; she was restrained/strapped down to a table and forced to have one against her will. Dany would not have made that decision for herself; she was not given a choice. The simple reality is that the availability of abortion on demand and the fact that it is acceptable to many people make this type of incident much more common than it should be.

Many fathers and husbands who are reading this book—some of whom may have also experienced the pain of abortion by finding out that a life they helped to create was cut short—have likely felt heartbreak as well. While our government would have you believe that they play no role and have no say in the choice of abortion, they actually play a pivotal role in preserving the life of their unborn child. Dany's child's father wanted to raise his child, and he was devastated when the opportunity was taken from him. The damage done was irreparable in his eyes, and he ended the relationship with Dany. Not only did she lose her precious child, but she also lost the man she loved.

Genetically, a child is just as much a part of the father as he is of the mother, but under the law a child's father does not have to consent to an abortion or even be informed that they have an unborn child. A mother can legally choose to abort her baby without giving any notice to the father whatsoever. In our society, men are frequently blamed for not standing up and taking responsibility for their actions. But what if they are not even given the chance to try?

While the onus is certainly upon men to stand up to gain rights for their unborn children, it is also important to note that great responsibility comes along with those rights. This includes accepting the consequences of their actions and helping to support the woman they slept with and their child if she gets pregnant. The greatest model for raising a family is the context of a biblical marriage, where both the husband and the wife depend on God to lead them.

Women need emotional, financial, physical, and spiritual support during pregnancy, knowing that the man is there to help them, and children need their fathers to help raise them. Men who are doing a good job of supporting their women and children should certainly be applauded, as their job is not an easy one. However, for those of you who are not embracing their responsibilities, I urge you to be the men God has called you to be.

Another issue that Dany's story addresses is the feeling of remorse following abortion. Both Dany and her child's father grieved the loss of their baby, as many parents do after abortions. While pro-abortion organizations might have women believe that the choice is theirs alone and that remorse is not and should not be an issue following abortion, as you can see in Dany's story that was not the case at all. She is pained by the abortion decades later, very much due to the fact that she never wanted it in the first place. In a few chapters you will also read about another friend of mine, named Kelcey, who made the decision to have an abortion in her teenage years and has deeply regretted it ever since.

Chapter 10

KERMIT GOSNELL

Emily LaBonte

Kermit Gosnell was an abortionist in inner-city Philadelphia who practiced for more than 30 years, routinely inducing the delivery of live, post-viability infants and snipping the backs of their necks with scissors to ensure fetal demise after delivery. He was eventually charged with first-degree murder on three counts and sentenced to three life sentences without the possibility of parole.

In the documentary *3801 Lancaster: American Tragedy*, a young woman who was raped initially went to Gosnell's clinic to have an abortion, but she changed her mind. She says that Gosnell restrained her and sedated her after she told him she did not want to move forward with the procedure. Before she went unconscious, she remembers Gosnell screaming at her to stop being a little baby as he pounded on her legs. When she woke up, she knew she was no longer pregnant.

According to the documentary, he frequently performed abortions on minors who were brought in by guardians who forced them to have the procedure. One of those teenage girls was taken to Gosnell's clinic by her grandmother to have an abortion, and she reported to *ABC News* that after she told Gosnell that she did not want to have the abortion he ripped off her clothes, slapped her, restrained her, sedated her, and performed the abortion against her consent.[34]

In his Grand Jury report, an incident is described in which he attempted to perform another abortion on an unwilling mother. He initiated a two- to three-day abortion procedure by dilating her cervix with laminaria (seaweed sticks used to dilate the cervix). She changed her mind about going through with the abortion after Gosnell told her that he burned aborted fetuses, but he refused to reverse what he had started. He also said that he would not refund the $1,300 she had paid him for the procedure. She went to the hospital and had the procedure successfully reversed. When she testified before the Grand Jury, her baby was starting kindergarten.[35]

Gosnell was allowed to practice like this in inner-city Philadelphia for more than 30 years without consequence, until he was arrested for an entirely different reason: drug trafficking. The lack of cleanliness of his clinic, the apparent lack of safety, and his malpractice had been reported on multiple occasions, but no follow-up actions had been taken. The Grand Jury report details how the Pennsylvania

Department of Health, the Pennsylvania Department of State, the Philadelphia Department of Health, and other doctors allowed this to keep happening for decades without consequence.[36] The report states:

> We discovered that Pennsylvania's Department of Health has deliberately chosen not to enforce laws that should afford patients at abortion clinics the same safeguards and assurances of quality health care as patients of other medical service providers. Even nail salons in Pennsylvania are more closely monitored for client safety.[37]

The report details that the Department of Health knew about the unsafe practices of Gosnell yet did absolutely nothing. They performed no inspections at all between 1993 and 2010—not even in response to complaints that were filed, 22-year-old Semika Shaw's death, or an ambulance that was called in response to another dying patient named Karnamaya Mongar.

Law enforcement was completely insufficient in protecting these women, late-term fetuses (at or beyond 24 weeks), and infants who were aborted alive. The Department of State did not investigate Gosnell after a complaint was filed when he perforated a woman's cervix, bowel, and uterus during an abortion. Philadelphia Department of Public Health superiors ignored their employees' alerts that something terrible was going on at Gosnell's clinic; the second alert was filed one month prior to the death of Karnamaya Mongar.

Many fellow doctors treating patients for complications following abortions that were performed by Gosnell also did not report the malpractice they saw (though some did). This brings to light how poorly abortion clinics are being monitored by our government officials and how easily unethical medical practice can take place and go on uninterrupted.

At any moment, wanted children could still be taken from their mothers in a gruesome way, and women could still be suffering completely avoidable complications. Certainly, this is not the standard of care, and most physicians of all specialties abide by the Hippocratic Oath, but we live in a fallen world. Unfortunately, there is no way to determine how frequently these situations are occurring because the facilities are not being monitored appropriately. While unacceptable, this is the current reality. Many government officials and politicians have the agenda of protecting and furthering abortion laws without considering the protection of the women or fetuses that those laws impact. I urge you, my fellow Christians, to stand up for the sanctity of life.

Chapter 11

ADOPTION

Emily LaBonte

I f you are a believer and find yourself in the situation of an unintended pregnancy, I urge you to consider adoption. Carrying a child whom a woman will not be keeping is one of the most difficult, yet loving and selfless, things anyone could ever do—it saves the life of the child and gives another couple a chance to be parents who might not otherwise be able to. As believers, we should do a better job of loving, encouraging, and supporting one another when we are in need. Let us not judge one another; rather, let us lend a helping hand when it is needed.

I recently heard one of the most beautiful stories. My mom emailed it to me because she knew that I was writing this book, but she did not know that I had decided to write this chapter the very same day! Again, the Lord has provided every step of the way for this book to be written.

Joy Villa is a singer and songwriter who has a beautiful story, and I think we can all learn from her courage and selflessness. This is what she said after being encouraged by her nurse to have an abortion:

. . . But when I was violently thrown against the wall by the baby's father while heavily pregnant, I knew I needed a real solution. My baby deserved so much better. That's when I made the most difficult and important decision of my life: I decided to carry my baby to term and then give her up for adoption to a loving family. I put her life over mine. It wasn't easy. Every day was a struggle. Ask any woman: Pregnancy is extraordinarily difficult, especially without family by your side. But my faith in God—and my love for my baby—gave me all the strength I needed to survive. I found an adoption agency that helped me every step of the way, including taking care of my day to day living expenses. We placed my baby with a loving, caring family in an "open adoption," which meant I could still be involved in her life. I have a growing and wonderful relationship with my daughter today, (who calls me "Mama Joy"!) because of my decision to choose life.[38]

Joy brings up an interesting alternative: the concept of open versus closed adoption. Joy personally chose an open adoption so that she can have an ongoing relationship with her daughter, which is wonderful. There are some women who may choose not to do that if it seems too painful, and that is okay as well. If you do not want to, you do not have to see your child again, and this is known as a closed adoption. Both are wonderful and selfless options for an individual to choose.

Another point worth mentioning is the fact that adopting parents help the birth mothers with expenses, if needed. Carrying a baby to term, birthing that baby in a hospital, and offering the baby for adoption should not financially burden the birth mother. According to the Adoption Network,

> If a Birth Parent has no medical insurance or means to pay for medical expenses, they can apply for Medicaid. If they do not qualify, the Adoptive Parent(s) may help pay for medical and hospital bills. Some states allow for the Adoptive Parents to temporarily assist with living expenses such as rent, food, transportation to and from doctor's appointments or legal and court appointments, and maternity clothes. State laws allow payments for housing for a limited time prior to and after birth, and are typically made directly to the landlord or once receipts are provided by the Birth Parent(s). State regulations dictate when and for how long they may provide such assistance.[39]

Some may choose abortion due to the fear that their baby would not be adopted. However, there are so many families waiting to adopt in the United States that this would not likely be an issue. There are some couples who desperately want children but cannot have them, and the selfless act of carrying a baby to term gives them that opportunity.

According to the Adoption Network,

> There are no national statistics on how many people are waiting to adopt, but experts estimate it is somewhere between one and two million couples. Every year there are about 1.3 million abortions. Only 4 percent of women with unwanted pregnancies place their children through adoption.[40]

With these startling statistics, we can understand that many couples who want children will likely never be able to have them unless they look abroad for a child to adopt. However, it would seem that adopting abroad is becoming more challenging as well, due to increasing restrictions. "While domestic adoption continues to grow, international adoption has declined significantly over the past several years, with just 7,092 adoptions in 2013, down from 8,668 in 2012, 9,319 in 2011 and 11,058 in 2010."[41] If there were fewer abortions, then more couples desiring adoption would have that dream fulfilled—it is simply a matter of supply and demand. The demand is currently being unfulfilled, largely due to abortion.

There are certain stigmas associated with putting a child up for adoption, such as a birth mother feeling as though she has failed as a parent. I came across a heartwarming video of a young man thanking his birth mother for giving him life and putting him up for adoption. He says,

> I've heard a lot of stories where women who have given up kids for adoption feel really guilty and sometimes it seems like a cowardly thing . . . but as someone who was adopted, from my point of view it's the total opposite. You've given someone the gift of life, you've sacrificed your body (your life) for someone who in 12 months you won't even know them. I'd love to be able to look my birth mother in the eye and just say how thankful I am.[42]

The truth is that there are many people who would say the same thing. According to the Adoption Network, there are 1.5 million adopted children in the United States today, and I am sure most of them would be thankful to their birth mothers for not aborting them and for giving them the gift of life.

Someone else also sacrificed His body selflessly so that we could all be adopted into the family of God as believers. As Paul points out in Romans 8:14–17,

> For all who are led by the Spirit of God are sons of God. For you did not receive the spirit of slavery to fall back into fear, but you have

received the Spirit of adoption as sons, by whom we cry, "Abba! Father!" The Spirit himself bears witness with our spirit that we are children of God, and if children, then heirs—heirs of God and fellow heirs with Christ, provided we suffer with him in order that we may also be glorified with him.

What a beautiful metaphor! Birth mothers choosing adoption for their children can be compared to our Savior himself! If you have considered or utilized adoption services, please do not feel condemnation for offering your child the chance to live. In His perfect plan from the beginning, God chose to adopt us as His children, and from the beginning Jesus Christ knew He would sacrifice His own body so we could be adopted. How beautiful! The sacrifice that you make for your child can be likened to the sacrifice Christ made (His on an eternal scale, of course)—Christ gave us life, just as a mother who chooses to utilize adoption can give her child life by sacrificing her body and carrying the child to term.

Chapter 12

KELCEY'S STORY

Emliy LaBonte (with Kelcey)

I first met Kelcey at church more than a year ago, and she has become a dear friend to me. She is kind, honest, and faithful. I first heard her story at a ladies' Bible study one Saturday morning, and I knew the Lord was leading me to write about her story in this book, but I did not yet know to what extent. Then, several months later, she told us at Bible study about a dream she had. I knew then what part her story would play.

Women have abortions, and there are consequences to that decision, just as with any other act of disobedience to the Lord. Hebrews 12:6 says, "For the Lord disciplines the one he loves, and chastises every son whom he receives." However, the Word is also very clear that God forgives, and He does not require us to clean up our act before He forgives us!

In Romans 5:8 we read, "God shows his love for us in that while we were still sinners, Christ died for us." He longs to set us free from the burdens we carry! In John 8:36 Jesus declares, "So if the Son sets you free, you will be free indeed." His love never fails and will never leave us.

Paul so beautifully asserts in Romans 8:38–39, "For I am sure that neither death nor life, nor angels nor rulers, nor things present nor things to come, nor powers, nor height nor depth, nor anything else in all creation, will be able to separate us from the love of God in Christ Jesus our Lord."

Kelcey's story is one of healing! God healed her from a heavy burden that she was carrying, and He can do the same thing for anyone who will seek after Him! I invite you to read her story, below:

When I was growing up, I was a very nervous, angst-filled teenager. I found myself coping with my feelings by using drugs and alcohol. I did not grow up with a solid father figure for most of my early upbringing, and I did not have a good relationship with my mother. I met the manager at my former workplace when I was just 16 years old. We became friends and had a cordial relationship, and I knew that he had a 9-year-old daughter but had little to do with her. One night after work, he needed a ride home, so I gave him a ride. When we got to his house, he said that he had something for me inside, so I went in with him. We went to his room, and he immediately locked the door. He turned off the lights, and it was a very uncomfortable situation. It was immediately evident what he was expecting. By this time, I was 17 years old and did not have a strong opinion about myself, and I certainly did not know how to stand up for myself in a situation like this. It was my first time having sex with anyone. It was a very painful and horrible experience. From that, I became pregnant, which I didn't think was possible because my menstrual cycles were so irregular. I realized that I was pregnant when I was about six weeks along, according to an app on my phone. When I took a pregnancy test, it was positive. My manager did not want another child, and I didn't want to raise a child without a father figure. I felt like I was following in my mother's footsteps because my mom was 17 years old when she was pregnant with me, and I did not want the same situation for my child. I didn't think I had another option aside from abortion. My manager took me to Planned Parenthood to have the procedure. I remember that they did not confirm the pregnancy in any way. I was tiny and not showing, so I guess they didn't feel like they needed to check how far along I was. After all, I couldn't have been that far along at all because of my size. I told them that I learned I was pregnant from a home pregnancy test, and they had me sign some paperwork but didn't really tell me what they were giving me or what was going to happen.

Then they handed me the abortion pills. By this time, I was 18 years old (technically an adult), and I did not have to let my parents know at all, so my mom was totally unaware of what was going on. I remember feeling very nauseated after the first round of medication, and I was not in a good place mentally. When I took the last abortion pill, I took it with four Xanax pills so I could sleep the rest of the day. After it happened, I forced myself to move on mentally because I didn't want to think about it. I knew I made a mistake, and I didn't want to do that again. I always wanted a family, but I just didn't think I could do it at that point. I didn't feel like I had another option. I did not think I could talk to my mom about it, and I knew she would be really angry with me. I felt so alone . . . like I had absolutely no one to turn to.

I grew up very confused about the Christian faith and didn't really want to be a part of it. I saw hypocrisy around me and didn't understand how people could claim to believe one thing and then live their lives another way. I was at a party with my mom, and one of her friends snuck me vodka and cranberry drinks. I got drunk and started sobbing about what happened and told my mom's friend that I had an abortion; she immediately went and told my mom, and it caused a big scene. Mom got angry and then made me go to a Christian counselor. I just couldn't deal with it at the time. I didn't want to go, and I didn't feel like it was helping anyway. I was not a Christian at the time. Christianity was shoved down my throat, but I didn't have a personal relationship with Jesus.

I have regretted the abortion in many ways. For years afterward, I hated myself, I hurt myself, I put myself in terrible situations, and I had horrible thoughts about myself. It took a long time to realize and truly process what I had done. Once I became pregnant with my daughter, it became real. The first few months of pregnancy with my daughter were really hard. I felt unworthy to be a mom, and I didn't feel like I deserved it. Now that I have her, she is a picture of God's grace for me. It took me a long time to realize that God still loves me and forgives me. I know that I messed up and made a horrible decision; however, God still loves me—so much so that He fulfilled my heart's biggest desire of having a family.

When I was about 22 years old, I started going to Christian women's retreats. I felt so unworthy of God's forgiveness. I felt like I had messed up so much that I couldn't obtain His forgiveness. One of the women at the retreat posed a question for me: Is the cross not good enough for you? I had to sit and think . . . why isn't Jesus' blood enough for me? I should be able to forgive myself. His love is enough for anyone else, and I'd forgive anyone that did the same things I had done. It was a long process to accept His love, forgiveness, and grace in my life. It took a lot of diving into the Word and surrounding myself with godly women to help guide me and speak life into me. For so long, I applied my own characteristics to God. I grew up with no father figure for most of my early childhood, and when my stepdad came around, I wanted nothing to do with him, even though he was the one who actually stuck around. Since I had no earthly dad, I didn't think God would want me or want to have a relationship with me, either—I placed that baggage on God. It took a long time to realize that I was applying earthly, absent-father characteristics to an ever-present, holy God, and that doesn't make sense. God is bigger than anything I can imagine. It was hard to think of God for who He is when I didn't have the best earthly father relationship. With time, after reading the Bible and surrounding myself with other believers, I have finally realized that I am forgiven and redeemed. It has taken a lot of time to get where I am today. There are still hard days, and the enemy does remind me frequently, but I can cling to the fact that I am forgiven.

God made His forgiveness very real for me through a dream that I had just a few months ago, and I'd like to share that dream. I was in a dark place and could see nothing around me, and all of a sudden, I could sense a light behind me. When I turned around, I saw Jesus on the cross, glowing brightly. As I looked around, I felt peaceful. But then I saw myself, and as I looked closer, I saw all of these horrible labels covering my body and felt so much shame. There were societal labels and labels I put on myself—all of them negative, terrible words, such as whore, unforgiveable, and sinner. Most of these were things I thought about myself, but there were also terms that society labels people after they have abortions. Then, I saw Jesus taking these labels off of me and placing them upon himself. He was telling me in this dream that I don't need to bear that weight anymore because He has taken it from me. He was telling me that I am free from that. He was saying that He still loves me despite mistakes from my past, and He doesn't see me for those mistakes. He sees me as His beautiful child. It felt so real, and it was so beautiful. When I woke up, I could do nothing but weep and thank Him for His loving kindness. The heavy weight of those labels was gone. I woke up feeling a sense of freedom and peace from finally letting go of all of those things I had placed upon myself for so long. His forgiveness was made so tangible to me through that dream.

Kelcey's story is so beautiful, and it is one of restoration. Dear reader, if you have had an abortion, God will forgive you and does not see you for your mistakes. If you believe in your heart and confess with your mouth that Jesus Christ is your Savior, then you are forgiven; you are made new by His blood. Confess your sins to Him, and He promises to forgive you. You do not have to carry the heavy burden of shame because His yoke is easy, and His burden is light (Matthew 11:30). His blood is enough to cover all your sins; believe and trust Him, and He will make you whole.

Dear reader, if you have performed an abortion or assisted in that process, believe that the words above are true for you as well. Do not believe for one second that your sin is greater than anyone else's. God promises to forgive you. As King David wrote, "As far as the east is from the west, so far does he remove our transgressions from us" (Psalm 103:12). As Paul (a former persecutor of Christ) wrote in 1 Timothy 1:15, "The saying is trustworthy and deserving of full acceptance, that Christ Jesus came into the world to save sinners, of whom I am the foremost." No sin is out of reach for Christ's healing blood. Praise God!

Chapter 13

SO WHAT SHOULD A CHRISTIAN DO?

Dr. Steve Hammond

You have now come to the application portion of this book, which explains how to use the information we have provided herein. We have exposed exactly what happens when an abortion is performed and presented a scientific and theological defense of the premise that unborn children are human beings.

Before we offer suggestions, we should prepare you to face the ultimate enemy: fear. While unfiltered anger can make you do things you shouldn't, fear stops you from doing things that you *should*. We encounter fear when we feel alone in our opinions and when others gang up on us. The intimidation that the crowds will ridicule you (or, worse, verbally destroy you) can stop you from even beginning a conversation. This is especially true if the group seems to already agree with an opposing point of view. We can be afraid when we don't know enough to support our position or worry that we can't make a convincing argument. We fear being ridiculed or persecuted.

Church leaders and pastors fear losing congregants, so they often stay neutral on the subject of abortion. I encourage you to read Revelation 3:15–16, where God addresses the church at Laodicea. God would prefer that pastors defend a position that they hold, even if it is contrary to that of those in their congregation, than see them ignore the holocaust that surrounds them out of fear of losing members or prestige among their peers. Jesus addresses trying to remain neutral on a moral matter when we know what is right, and He says that He despises our being "lukewarm." I hate to imagine what "being spit out of His mouth" must be like (Revelation 3:16).

The antidote for fear is to remember the attributes of God: He is not vulnerable; He—and therefore His opinion—does not ever change; and He is omnipotent.

We may cower under the threat of those who support abortion on demand due to their sheer numbers and the lofty platforms (government and even some church hierarchy) that they occupy on this earth. God is not intimidated by either. His Word gives us His opinion on the matter, and I am reminded of the story of Elijah in 1 Kings 18. Can you imagine the intimidation he must have felt as he challenged the prophets of Baal to a contest—his God against 450 prophets of Baal and their gods?

Even Elijah's own people were of two opinions—they were trying to straddle the fence and worship

Baal and the God of Israel at the same time, and they were not on Elijah's side, at least before the contest. Two altars were built, with a sacrificial ox on each, and Elijah asked the prophets of Baal to have their gods bring down fire on the altar.

As they chanted, cut themselves, and went through all of their rituals, Elijah laughed and mocked them. (He was confident in his God.) Then he had them pour water all around his altar and soak it with still more water. God's fire consumed the entire altar, water and all, and the false prophets were killed. Even after seeing this display of power, Jezebel threatened to kill Elijah, and instead of relying on the same power that had consumed the altar Elijah was afraid and fled for his life.

Did God rebuke Elijah? No—He pursued him and sent angels to minister to him. We can understand through this passage that God is not only invulnerable to man's opinion, but He understands our weaknesses and fears and is patient and compassionate with us, as He was with Elijah; this should remind us to be of good courage.

The Bible makes innumerable references to the fact that God never changes. He is immutable. In Jeremiah 1:5, God states that before He formed Jeremiah in his mother's womb, He knew him and consecrated him as a prophet to the nations. There are two important points here. First, God knew Jeremiah before he was even conceived! This is a remarkable statement, and if it is true of Jeremiah it is true of every other human who has ever been conceived, including you and me.

Second, God had a plan for Jeremiah even before he was conceived. God has a plan for each of us, too, and equips us to be able to accomplish what He has designed us to do. Since God never changes, the fact that this declaration appears in the Old Testament in no way diminishes its applicability for teaching us about God's attributes. We can receive this truth about God's foreknowing you, me, and the baby in a pregnant woman's womb as confidently as we receive the truth that "God so loved the world, that he gave his only Son" (John 3:16).

Finally, God is omnipotent. If you lack courage or wisdom, ask Him for it. We don't have because we don't ask! We don't often think of the power of God. We can access that power through prayer—but not in the crass way in which some refer to channeling God's power to accomplish what they want. God is on the side of those who seek His face and desire to do His will, and He will provide the supernatural power of the Holy Spirit for you to accomplish His purpose. Do not fear, "for he who is in you is greater than he who is in the world" (1 John 4:4).

Pro-choice advocates will assert that a pro-life perspective should be private and not used in public debate. As a person who is pro-life, you may hear them say that you must not use your weight of influence to convince others that abortion is wrong or that it ends a human life. People will encourage you to turn your back on your convictions about abortion and take a middle ground that, by virtue of your silence in public, does not push back against abortion and the industry that promotes and provides it. In other words, they are telling you not to speak out on what your faith informs you is morally wrong. Before you cower at this demand, consider what John Piper had to say in a sermon titled "Love Your Unborn Neighbor":

> God says to us in America in the 21st century stained with the blood of millions of unborn babies, these words from Proverbs 24:11–12: "Rescue those who are being taken away to death; hold back those who are stumbling to the slaughter. If you say, 'Behold, we did not know this,' does not he who weighs the heart perceive it? Does not he who keeps watch over your soul know it, and will he not repay man according to his work?"[43]

We believe that the first thing a Christian who studies the issue of abortion should do is read and extend that study beyond this book. Start by reading the Bible and what it says about God's creation of man, and then explore the chapters and books following Genesis, which reveal His love of humanity, culminating in His giving His only Son for humankind. Pray for guidance by the Holy Spirit as you do so. You will find a God who promotes life, asks His children to submit (obey) in a loving response to this gift to us, and promises to guide us in all things. Seeking the character of God and what He loves and expects of us is the first duty of a Christian.

Second, Jesus asks those who would follow Him to take up their cross in doing so. This is the idea that instead of demanding rights we are to submit our will to His. This means that we are to give up our rights— not the privileges of salvation and living for eternity with Him, but the selfish rights born of our own will. Jesus promises a reward to all who will deny themselves these rights.

Of course, this collides head-on with the cultural belief that we are entitled to these rights and, in fact, deserve them. Therefore, we cannot expect non-believers to accept this premise; it will be rejected as foolishness. That should not deter us from promoting the basis of our belief that the selfish right to choose (in this case) is trumped by our understanding of God's view of life. Clearly, our audience is fellow Christians, as we encourage them to grow in their knowledge of God's will (which is found in His Word) and the wisdom to apply that knowledge.

Finally, if we are to be heard by the broader culture, we must always engage those who disagree with respect and love, even if they are not so generous. While it is imperative that we never back away or equivocate on truth, we can always engage with the love of Christ. It is very likely that few Christian skeptics or non-believers will receive the message of this book, especially on the initial presentation of this perspective. It has been my experience, however, that many who respond initially with rebuke or hostility come to later soften their tone and even return with questions. Be loving, but be persistent and patient. I have seen seeds that were planted in unlikely fields take root and bloom after a season of water and sunshine.

Planting seeds that challenge a person to consider the pro-life perspective can best be done by challenging a person who supports abortion with soul-searching questions. Rarely will you convince someone to reconsider their stance by arguing with them both sides of the equation. Debates usually result in both sides digging in and clinging harder to their beliefs or, worse, resorting to name-calling. While it is always good to be ready to respond thoughtfully and kindly to a question that is presented to you, any lull during a discussion allows you to pose questions of your own.

Challenging another person's thinking is best done by presenting a probing question. You may think of some of your own, but below are a few to get you started:

1. Should any person ever have the power of life or death over another person? If not, why does this not apply to a woman's choice to destroy a baby inside her womb?

2. If a mother can be prosecuted and even charged with murder for neglecting a child (such as leaving a child in a hot car during the summer), what is the difference if that same mother has her baby killed and removed from her womb one or two weeks before such an incident?

3. Shouldn't a woman be required to see an ultrasound picture of the baby inside her womb before agreeing to an abortion? If not, how can she fully grasp what she is doing enough to provide informed consent?

4. You were once an embryo inside your mother's womb. What if she had chosen abortion?

5. Would you consider the Holocaust and the American history of slavery morally wrong? If so, can you consider that even though abortion is largely socially acceptable (as were the Holocaust in Nazi Germany and slavery in American history), it may at the same time be morally wrong?

6. Is ensuring convenience for one person worth destroying the life of another person?

While none of these questions will likely result in a "Eureka!" moment for the other person, they may have a way of incubating over time and blossoming into a change of heart by getting them to think and question their own position. This is how public opinion—and ultimately the law governing abortion—will by changed in this country . . . one heart at a time.

For those who have had abortions or been affected by the abortion of someone close, I bring you good news. Jesus died for all sins that are confessed and given to Him. So many believers carry their past sins around with them when God promises to wash them as "white as snow." Such believers should offer not only a prayer of confession (if they were indeed culpable for the decision to abort) but a plea for forgiveness for not believing God and trusting His promise. There is no confessed sin that is unforgivable. We must share this message with those who are suffering unnecessarily and present it to those whose guilt and sins are unconfessed. The latter must be persuaded that there is a better way to live through trust in Christ.

Chapter 14

CLOSING PRAYER AND THOUGHTS

Dr. Steve Hammond and Emily LaBonte

We have covered a number of topics in this book surrounding abortion in an effort to equip you, dear Christian, with the information you need to be completely convinced that God views abortion as sinful. We have also provided information to enable you to speak out against this practice. We have presented you with practical ways to get involved to stand against abortion and help others in need (both in the previous chapter and again in Appendix B, to follow). At this time, our hearts turn to prayer. We need to stand united as one body of believers and blanket this issue with prayer. We need to pray that abortion would be no more, that lives would be saved, that women would be blessed for choosing life, and that God would receive all of the glory for these things happening. There is power in prayer. Join me in repeating this prayer often, speaking it out loud, and praying it together with like-minded believers:

Dear heavenly Father,

You are the maker of the heavens, the earth, and all of our individual souls, both born and unborn. Lord, you deserve all praise for the beautiful works of your hands! You alone are God and worthy of praise. You alone reserve the right to give and take away life. Lord, you are in total control! We pray that abortion would end, and while we do not know how this will come to be, we trust you, Father.

Lord, we pray over the church; we pray that the church would stand united against abortion, that it would be bold and full of truth and love. Lord, may the church no longer be influenced by the world; may the church influence the world for your glory and with your truth. May it be a bountiful resource for single moms who choose life.

Lord, we pray over individual Christians' hearts that are not fully convinced that abortion is wrong. We pray that their hearts would turn to the truth and that they would make a bold stand against abortion. Lord, every voice counts, and every voice can save a life.

Lord, we pray over government powers. May they stand against abortion. Lord, we pray that you would end this holocaust of unborn children and that you would convict the hearts of those who help to make our laws so that they would see the truth that abortion is wrong.

Lord, we pray against what Satan is doing in secular society, which is making abortion look appealing and worth boasting about. We pray that you would thwart this dark and deceptive scheme and that it would become absolutely distasteful, even in the eyes of the secular world. We know that abortion is sinful because it ends human lives that you call worthy of dying for.

Lord, we pray for women who are contemplating abortion. Please change their hearts so that they will choose life instead of death. Bless any new mother and be her provider.

Lord, we pray for every Christian who has already taken an anti-abortion stance. Show them how they can play a role in ending abortion, whether by talking to their pastors, praying, writing letters to their government officials, or just speaking the truth to their family and friends. Lord, show each of us the role we can play in ending this sinful practice.

Lord, heal those who have been affected by abortion. Show your grace and kindness to all who desire your forgiveness for having or having performed abortions.

Lord, more than anything else, we pray that your name may be glorified, no matter what. We pray for your will to be done. We love you with all of our hearts.

In Jesus' name we pray,
Amen

APPENDIX A

FETAL DEVELOPMENT CHART

This chart shows vulnerability of the fetus to defects throughout 38 weeks of pregnancy.*

● = Most common site of birth defects

PERIOD OF THE OVUM		PERIOD OF THE EMBRYO						PERIOD OF THE FETUS				
Weeks 1-2	Week 3	Week 4	Week 5	Week 6	Week 7	Week 8	Week 12	Week 16	Weeks 20–36	Week 38

Period of early embryo development and implantation.

CNS
heart

eye
heart

eye
heart

eye

limbs

ear

teeth

ear
palate

external genitals

brain

external genitals

Central Nervous System (CNS)–Brain and Spinal Cord

Heart

Arms/Legs

Eyes

Teeth

Palate

External Genitals

Ears

Pregnancy loss

■ Period of development when major defects in bodily structure can occur.

▬ Period of development when major functional defects and minor structural defects can occur.

Adapted from Moore, 1993 and the National Organization on Fetal Alcohol Syndrome (NOFAS) 2009

*This fetal chart shows the 38 weeks of pregnancy. Since it is difficult to know exactly when conception occurs, health care providers calculate a woman's due date 40 weeks from the start of her last menstrual cycle.

161

APPENDIX B

J ust one final thought: Abortion is more accessible and acceptable today than ever before in history. After reading the pages of this book and Scripture from the Bible, are you convinced that abortion is wrong? If so, what are you going to do about it? Please consider utilizing the resources below to help you with next steps.

Suggested Resources and Ways to Get Involved

Whether you want to get involved in the fight against abortion, are a medical provider seeking resources to help your patients, or are suffering from the effects of abortion (personally or through someone you love), there are a number of resources designed to provide the support you need. While we recommend visiting these resources, we (and you) may not agree with everything they promote.

Resources for getting involved on a community or country level:

- *https://marchforlife.org*
- *https://40daysforlife.com*

- *https://www.nrlc.org/site/*
- *https://all.org/programs/?gclid=Cj0KCQiAtP_ iBRDGARIsAEWJA8jig8mjq24IrW5-mr2QCra PYAgTsvIC1lWqOiY982i9lRpTRqIC7OEaAr1x EALw_wcB*
- *https://www.senate.gov/reference/common/faq/ How_to_correspond_senators.htm*
- *https://www.house.gov/representatives/find- your-representative*

Resource for medical providers:

- *https://aaplog.org*

Resource for those hurting from the effects of abortion:

- *http://www.abortionrecoveryinternational.org/ home/tabid/55/Default.aspx*

If you want to lend a hand in your community, conduct an internet search for local pregnancy crisis centers to connect with new moms and offer your assistance. You can also get connected in a local church that promotes life or allow the Lord to use you as a change agent if your church does not already promote life.

ACKNOWLEDGMENTS

The authors would like to thank Dany, Kelcey, and Carrie Brown for their willingness to share their personal stories of grief and hardship. Their stories of overcoming hardship and grief will be a source of inspiration to thousands who read their accounts. They all agreed to let us use their real names or nickname to bolster their authenticity. We pray that God will bless them for their courage.

We dedicate this book to our respective families, especially our children and grandchildren. When we look at their faces, we see the indelible resemblance of ourselves, in much the same way God looks upon us and sees His image in us. As we love our children unconditionally, in ways that we will never completely understand in this life, God loves us even more.

For the gift of expression that God bestowed on two totally inexperienced writers, we are humbly grateful. Our prayers that He would speak through us and help us find assistance and encouragement for our task were answered. Thanks to David Sanford, our publicist, and to Tim Beals and his team at Credo House Publishers, for helping us navigate the world of publishing and polishing our manuscript. Thank you, Mary Anne Hensley, for your hard work on the front end with the first round of editing.

We want to thank our pastors Eugene Brandt, Fellowship Bible Church, Jackson, Tennessee, and Jon LaBonte and Steve Witt, The Well Church, Henderson, Nevada, who offered advice, support, and encouragement along the way. They are in our prayers every day.

Steve Hammond, MD
Emily LaBonte, FNP-BC

ENDNOTES

1   Characteristics of U.S. Abortion Patients in 2014 and Changes Since 2008. (2016, June 10). Retrieved June 7, 2019, from *https://www.guttmacher.org/report/characteristics-us-abortion-patients-2014*.

2   Beckwith, F., & Koukl, G. (1998). *Relativism: Feet Firmly Planted in Mid-Air*. Grand Rapids, MI: Baker Pub. Group.

3   Sproul, R. C. (2010). *Abortion: a Rational Look at an Emotional Issue*. Orlando, FL: Reformation Trust Pub.

4   Stuart, D. K. (2006). *Exodus* (Vol 2). Nashville: Broadman & Holman Publishers.

5   Schwarz, S. D. (1990). *The Moral Question of Abortion*. Chicago: Loyola Univ. Press.

6   An Overview of Abortion Laws | Guttmacher Institute. (n.d.). Retrieved June 7, 2019, from *https://www.guttmacher.org/state-policy/explore/overview-abortion-laws*.

7   Parental Drug Use as Child Abuse. (n.d.). Retrieved June 7, 2019, from *https://www.childwelfare.gov/pubPDFs/drug exposed.pdf*.

8   18 U.S. Code § 3596 - Implementation of a sentence of . . . (n.d.). Retrieved June 7, 2019, from *https://www.law.cornell.edu/uscode/text/18/3596*.

9   Fetal Homicide State Laws - National Conference of State . . . (n.d.). Retrieved June 7, 2019, from *http://www.ncsl.org/research/health/fetal-homicide-state-laws.aspx*.

10 Sex-Selective Abortion Bans—A Disingenuous New Strategy to . . . (n.d.). Retrieved June 7, 2019, from *https:// www.guttmacher.org/news-release/2012/sex-selective- abortion-bans-disingenuous-new-strategy-limit-womens- access-abortion.*

11 Induced Abortion in the United States. (2017, October 20). Retrieved June 7, 2019, from *https://www.guttmacher. org/fact-sheet/induced-abortion-united-states.*

12 Lubbe, Rachel. "The Silent Scream (Full Length)." YouTube. January 27, 2012. Accessed June 7, 2019. https:// www.youtube.com/watch?v=gON-8PP6zgQ.

13 Zail, C. P. (n.d.). Protecting the Unborn: the Pain-Capable Unborn Child Protection Act. *Amac Advantage,* (Winter 2018).

14 Sex Offenses and Offenders — bjs.gov. (n.d.). Retrieved June 7, 2019, from *http://www.bjs.gov/content/pub/pdf/ SOO.PDF.*

15 "Breast Cancer During Pregnancy." National Cancer Institute. Accessed June 7, 2019. *https://www.cancer. gov/types/breast/patient/pregnancy-breast-treatment- pdq#_164.*

16 Clark, R. M., and T. Chua. "Breast Cancer and Pregnancy: The Ultimate Challenge." *Clinical Oncology* 1, no. 1 (1989): 11-18. doi:10.1016/s0936-6555(89)80004-4.

17 Hvistendahl, M. (2012). *Unnatural Selection: Choosing Boys over Girls, and the Consequences of a World Full of Men.* New York: Public Affairs.

18 Okeke, T., Ezenyeaku, C., & Ikeako, L. (2013). Retrieved June 7, 2019, from *https://www.ncbi.nlm.nih.gov/pmc/ articles/PMC3793431/.*

19 Reproductive Health. (2017, November 09). Retrieved June 7, 2019, from *https://www.cdc.gov/reproductivehealth/ maternalinfanthealth/pmss.html*.

20 Reasons U.S. Women Have Abortions: Quantitative and . . . (n.d.). Retrieved June 7, 2019, from *https://www. guttmacher.org/sites/default/files/pdfs/journals/3711005.pdf*.

21 Women's Experience with a 72-Hour Waiting Period for . . . (n.d.). Retrieved June 7, 2019, from *https://scholars.org/ brief/womens-experience-72-hour-waiting-period-abortion*.

22 Rogers, A. (n.d.). "Roe V. Wade: a Case of Deadly Deception." *Amac Advantage*, (Winter 2018).

23 AAPLOG. (2018, January). War on Hippocratic Conscience, Planned Parenthood Problems and Coleman Study on Coerced Abortion [E-mail].

24 An Overview of Abortion Laws. (2018, January 02). Retrieved June 7, 2019, from *https://www.guttmacher.org/ state-policy/explore/overview-abortion-laws*.

25 Coleman, P. K., Reardon, D. C., & Calhoun, B. C. (2012). Reproductive History Patterns and Long-Term Mortality Rates: a Danish, Population-Based Record Linkage Study. *The European Journal of Public Health, 23*(4), 569-574. doi:10.1093/eurpub/cks107

26 Johnson, A., & Lambert, C. (2014). *Unplanned: The Dramatic True Story of a Former Planned Parenthood Leader's Eye-Opening Journey Across the Life Line.* Carol Stream, IL: Tyndale House, Inc.

27 Progress, The Center for Medical. "Planned Parenthood Uses Partial-Birth Abortions to Sell Baby Parts." YouTube. July 14, 2015. Accessed June 7, 2019. https://www.youtube. com/watch?v=jjxwVuozMnU.

28 Abortion Complications. (n.d.). Retrieved June 7, 2019, from *http://aaplog.org/*.

29 "Woman with Down Syndrome Gives Awesome Pro-Life Speech at UN: "Please don't try to kill us all off." Retrieved June 7, 2019, from www.lifesitenews.com/news/down-syndrome-woman-blasts-abortion-genocide-in-un-speech-gets-a-standing-o.

30 *Does Abortion Really Prevent Child Abuse? - Mike Adams.* Retrieved June 7, 2019, from *https://townhall.com/columnists/mikeadams/2017/02/14/does-abortion-really-prevent-child-abuse-n2285323*.

31 Hammond, S., MD. (2019, January 31). [Telephone interview].

32 Preamble to the Declaration of Independence.

33 Willke, J. C., & Willke, B. (1991). *Abortion: Questions and Answers.* Cincinnati: Hayes. (p. 136).

34 "Philly Abortion Doc a 'Monster': Alleged Victim." [Television broadcast]. (n.d.).

35 *In the Court of Common Pleas First Judicial District of Pennsylvania Criminal Trial Division Report of the Grand Jury* (pp. 86–87, Rep. No. Misc. no. 0009901-2008). (2011).

36 *In the Court of Common Pleas First Judicial District of Pennsylvania Criminal Trial Division Report of the Grand Jury* (pp. 137–217, Rep. No. Misc. no. 0009901-2008). (2011).

37 *In the Court of Common Pleas First Judicial District of Pennsylvania Criminal Trial Division Report of the Grand Jury* (p. 137, Rep. No. Misc. no. 0009901-2008). (2011).

38 Joy Villa: Why I choose life over abortion—The incredible journey that began for me at 20. (n.d.). Retrieved June 7,

2019, from *http://www.foxnews.com/opinion/2018/01/31/ joy-villa-why-choose-life-over-abortion-incredible- journey-that-began-for-me-at-20.html.*

39   Do Adoptive Parents Provide Financial Support for a Birth Mother? (n.d.). Retrieved June 7, 2019, from *https:// adoptionnetwork.com/do-adoptive-parents-provide- financial-support-for-a-birth-mother.*

40   Adoption Statistics | Adoption Network. (n.d.). Retrieved June 7, 2019, from *https://adoptionnetwork.com/adoption- statistics.*

41   Domestic vs. International Adoption. (n.d.). Retrieved June 7, 2019, from *https://www.americanadoptions.com/ adopt/domestic_international.*

42   Jon, Ryan. "I've Never Met My Biological Mother." YouTube. May 07, 2017. Accessed June 7, 2019. *https:// www.youtube.com/watch?v=E_Zy3kQr-0w.*

43   Love Your Unborn Neighbor. Retrieved June 7, 2019, from *https://www.desiringgod.org/messages/love-your-unborn- neighbor.*

44   An Alcohol-Free Pregnancy Is the Best Choice for Your Baby. (n.d.). Retrieved June 7, 2019, from *https://www.cdc. gov/ncbddd/fasd/documents/fasdbrochure_final.pdf.*